Numeracy and

A practical introduction to the application and interpretation of financial and statistical information in organisations

Peter and Kathleen Fearns

HODDER AND STOUGHTON
LONDON SYDNEY AUCKLAND TORONTO

Peter Fearns — Principal, Burton-on-Trent Technical College
Kathleen Fearns — Lecturer, Derby College of Further Education

British Library Cataloguing in Publication Data

Fearns, Peter
Numeracy and finance: a practical introduction to the application and interpretation of financial and statistical information in organisations.
1. Corporations—Finance—Statistical methods.
I. Title. II. Fearns, Kathleen
519.5'024658 HG4027.15

ISBN 0 340 37004 1

Printed and bound in Great Britain for Hodder and Stoughton Educational, a division of Hodder and Stoughton Ltd, Mill Road, Dunton Green, Sevenoaks, Kent, by Page Bros (Norwich) Ltd.

Typeset by Macmillan India Ltd., Bangalore 25.

Contents

Preface v

1 Revision of the four rules 1
2 Fractions and decimals 5
3 Percentages and ratios 17
4 Equations 28
5 Collection of data and tabulation 43
6 Diagrammatic presentation of data 53
7 Graphs and scatter diagrams 65
8 Averages 81
9 Index numbers 96
10 Purpose and development of accounting 102
11 Profit and loss account and balance sheet 105
12 Accounting conventions 121
13 Interpretation and application of accounting information 131
14 Information technology and business operations 147
15 The organisation of information processing 156

Glossary of technical terms 164

Twenty assignments 171

Acknowledgements

Tables and diagrams from *Social Trends* and *Regional Trends* are reproduced with the permission of the Controller of Her Majesty's Stationery Office.

Preface

Numeracy and Finance is an introductory text to business statistics and finance, and as such is useful to all students on the BTEC National Business Studies courses, and for any student taking up studies in business or management. The aim of the book is to provide a basic text which meets the contemporary course requirements of BTEC, particularly in relation to the core module, *Finance*. The Business and Technician Education Council have been critical of the narrow base on which numeracy and finance have been taught on business studies courses, and they have asked for greater relevance, more practical realism and more integration of the subjects. This book aims to give a broad foundation in numeracy skills, to facilitate the development of problem solving skills, and to give students a working knowledge of statistical and financial methods. In order to meet BTEC's requirements the book is structured so that it explains the basic concepts in numeracy and finance, and it also gives relevant examples and integrated practical assignments.

The data which is used in the text is taken exclusively from two Government publications: *Social Trends* and *Regional Trends*. These are references which are published annually, and are available from most libraries. The text is a good guide to how the publications can be used in business studies; and, since it is a guide, it encourages teachers and students to obtain and use up-to-date information. Each chapter includes worked examples as well as problems for students to solve. It is intended that the worked examples and exercises provide an appropriate range of tasks and applications which are relevant to the students' experience. A glossary of technical terms has been included to enable students to obtain quickly a brief explanation of the concepts in finance and data processing.

Twenty assignments are set in the book and they have been specifically designed to integrate with other business studies modules. The assignments vary but they do have some common features: they require individual work and group work, they test problem solving skills, and the student's response or solution has to be aimed at a specified person or specified group of people. The assignments, like the whole text, are not designed to provide a comprehensive course in numeracy and finance, but to provide support material and support explanations which the teacher can mould to meet local needs.

1 Revision of the four rules

1.1 Introduction

The four rules are the four simplest arithmetic operations: addition (+), subtraction (−), multiplication (×) and division (÷). It is extremely important to understand the principles which govern these basic operations and the purpose of this chapter is to revise and clarify their uses.

Most students of business studies will be very familiar with the four simple arithmetic operations and probably will not need to do the revision exercises in this chapter. However, it would be wise for all students to complete the Exercise 1.1.

Exercise 1.1 is a simple diagnostic test. If a student is not able to answer every question correctly then they should study the rest of the chapter. The answers are given on page 218.

Exercise 1.1

(*a*) $56 + 85 + 43$	(*b*) $67 - 45$	(*c*) $18 - 6 + 37$
(*d*) 58×7	(*e*) $153 \div 9$	(*f*) $567 - 238$
(*g*) 201×19	(*h*) $3115 \div 35$	(*i*) $7 \times 5 \times 4$
(*j*) $4 \times 18 \div 3$	(*k*) $-8 - 12$	(*l*) -6×3
(*m*) -5×-9	(*n*) $7 + 11 \times 3$	(*o*) $15 - 4 \times 9$
(*p*) $6(5)$	(*q*) $4(8 + 2)$	(*r*) $6(9 - 4)$
(*s*) $-3(6 - 2)$	(*t*) $(2 + 8)(6 - 3)$	(*u*) $7 - 5 \times 6 + 9$
(*v*) $-8(56 + 19)$	(*w*) $147 \times 65 \div 5$	(*x*) $-6(589 + 269) \div 3$

1.2 Addition (+)

The purpose of addition is to find the sum of two or more numbers. For example:

$$4 = 4$$
$$4 + 18 = 22$$
$$4 + 6 + 18 = 28$$

The plus sign (+) in front of a number means that that number is positive. It is assumed that if a number does not have a sign then it is a positive number. In the example given above even though the number 4 does not have a sign it has, quite correctly, been added to the other numbers.

Exercise 1.2

(*a*) $5+3+6$	(*b*) $8+13+9$	(*c*) $56+85+43$
(*d*) $5+87+562$	(*e*) $51+784+943$	(*f*) $555+146$
(*g*) $6982+235$	(*h*) $3+78952+490$	(*i*) $106+98+5309$

1.3 Subtraction (−)

When a number is subtracted from another number then the result is the difference between the two numbers. For example:

$$13-4 = 9$$
$$5-9 = -4$$
$$256-377 = -121$$

The minus sign (−) in front of a number means that the number is negative, in other words less than 0. A positive number is always greater than a negative number. For example 23 is greater than −564 and 2 is greater than −3298. Negative numbers often occur in business, particularly in accounting. For example a loss by a firm is a negative number as is an overdraft in a bank account.

Exercise 1.3

(*a*) $8-5$	(*b*) $12-75$	(*c*) $456-231$
(*d*) $520-789$	(*e*) $14-5691$	(*d*) $321-8216$

1.4 Addition of positive and negative numbers

When a problem includes both positive and negative numbers then one method of finding the total is first to add the positive numbers and then add the negative numbers; then the sum of negative numbers can be subtracted from the sum of the positive numbers. For example:

$$8-6+4+7-3 = 19-9 = 10$$
$$45-86-22-74+13 = 58-182 = -124$$
$$-856+2314-65-7561+4803 = -8482+7117 = -1365$$

Exercise 1.4

(*a*) $12 - 86 - 70$	(*b*) $-23 + 900 - 53$	(*c*) $456 - 78 + 1432$
(*d*) $-895 + 12 - 42$	(*e*) $7803 + 21 - 6549$	(*f*) $1567 - 980 + 65$
(*g*) $36598 - 45 - 85$	(*h*) $-522 + 509 - 05$	(*i*) $200 + 9873 - 55$

1.5 Multiplication (×)

Multiplication is repeated addition. If, for instance, we multiply 4×3 then that is the same as adding 3 four times or adding 4 three times, for example:

$$3 + 3 + 3 + 3 = 12$$
$$4 + 4 + 4 = 12$$
$$4 \times 3 = 12$$
$$3 \times 4 = 12$$

Multiplication tables provide an easy method of solving multiplication problems. Obviously electronic calculators go even further to simplify the problem. But it would be unwise to rely entirely on calculators. Students' skills in numeracy are improved when mental calculation is used. Thoughtful calculation can help you to understand the relationship between figures.

You should be able to solve the following questions without using a calculator. It would help if:

(*1*) You revised the multiplication tables.
(*2*) You examined each question to see whether a short-cut or easy calculation is within the question.

Exercise 1.5

(*a*) 3×8	(*b*) $5 \times 11 \times 21$	(*c*) $12 \times 15 \times 5$
(*d*) 25×78	(*e*) 18×256	(*f*) 92×122
(*g*) 105×236	(*h*) 279×46	(*i*) 368×590

1.6 Division (÷)

Division is the reverse of multiplication. It is the process of dividing a number into equal parts. For example:

since $30 = 6 + 6 + 6 + 6 + 6$ then $30 \div 5 = 6$
since $30 = 5 + 5 + 5 + 5 + 5 + 5$ then $30 \div 6 = 5$

In this example both 5 and 6 are known as factors of 30; in other words they are numbers which when multiplied together give us the product 30. The other factors of 30 are 3 and 10, 2 and 15, and 1 and 30.

It is important that you know the multiplication tables so that you can work out the factors in a division problem.

Exercise 1.6

(*a*) $96 \div 8$	(*b*) $125 \div 5$	(*c*) $432 \div 16$
(*d*) $615 \div 15$	(*e*) $1161 \div 43$	(*f*) $529 \div 23$
(*g*) $765 \div 45$	(*h*) $6944 \div 124$	(*i*) $27272 \div 487$

1.7 Order of operations

In a problem where there are several different types of operations it is important to work them out in the correct order; otherwise an incorrect answer will be obtained. For example:

$$5 + 3 \times 2 = 5 + 6 = 11$$

Note that

$$5 + 3 \times 2 \text{ does } \textit{not} \text{ equal } 8 \times 2$$

Many problems show operations which are in brackets. This simply means that the content of the brackets must be worked out first. For example:

$$17 - (6 + 2) = 17 - 8 = 9$$

The correct order of operations is:

brackets, multiplication and division, addition and subtraction.

For example:

$$\begin{aligned} & 24 - 3(33 + 12) \div 5 - (11 - 6) \\ &= 24 - 3 \times 45 \div 5 - 5 \\ &= 24 - 3 \times 9 - 5 \\ &= 24 - 27 - 5 \\ &= -8 \end{aligned}$$

Do note that the multiplication sign is often left out when brackets are used so $3(33 + 12)$ is the same as $3 \times (33 + 12)$. In some instances the multiplication sign ($\times$) can be confusing and so a dot ($\cdot$) is used.

Exercise 1.7

(*a*) $12 + 2 \times 4 - 6$	(*b*) $14 - 10 \div 5 - 3$
(*c*) $6 + 5(4 - 1)$	(*d*) $25 - 14 \div (2 + 5)$
(*e*) $2(27 - 6) \div 7 - 1$	(*f*) $-2(6 + 13) - 7(2 - 9)$
(*g*) $(19 - 4) \div 3 + 4 - 3 \times 2$	(*h*) $7 + 2(5 \times 3 + 9) \div 3 - (4 - 6)$
(*i*) $-4 - (18 \div 3 - 3 \times 7) \div 5$	(*j*) $3(6 + 34) \div (15 - 3)$

2 Fractions and decimals

2.1 Introduction to fractions

A fraction is part of a whole number. Fractions are useful in business when we want to divide things up. For example if a partnership is owned by three people who want to share the profits equally then each would get 1 ÷ 3 which is one-third (1/3).

It is rare in the real world of business for things to be divided so easily. For example, in the partnership example given above the partners could decide that partner A has one share, partner B has five shares, and partner C has eleven shares. This adds up to a total of seventeen shares. In this case the fractions are:

$$\text{Partner A} = \frac{1}{17}$$

$$\text{Partner B} = \frac{5}{17}$$

$$\text{Partner C} = \frac{11}{17}$$

One purpose of this chapter is to review how the four rules apply to fractions and to give you a basis for understanding the application of fractions in later chapters.

2.2 Numerator and denominator

In the examples of fractions given above you will see that each fraction consists of two parts. The top part is known as the numerator and the bottom part is the denominator. So in the fraction 11/17, 11 is the numerator and 17 is the denominator. If we multiply or divide the numerator and denominator of a fraction by the same number the value of the fraction remains the same. For example 10/15 = 2/3 = 4/6 = 30/45 and so on.

In all of the examples given so far the numerator is smaller than the denominator; these are called *proper fractions*. Where the numerator is greater than the denominator the fractions are called *improper fractions.* A number consisting of a whole number and a fraction, such as $3\frac{5}{8}$ is called a *mixed number.* It can be converted to an improper fraction by the following steps (it is important to notice that the denominator does not change):

(1) multiply $3 \times 8 = 24$;
(2) add $24 + 5 = 29$;
(3) the fraction becomes 29/8.

An improper fraction can be converted to a proper fraction by seeing how many times the denominator can be divided into the numerator; this will give you the whole number. The remainder is then placed over the denominator. For example:

In the improper fraction 25/7,
7 can be divided into 25 three times;
∴ the whole number is 3,
the remainder is 4,
and so the fraction becomes $3\frac{4}{7}$.

2.3 Addition and subtraction of fractions

Where fractions have a similar or common denominator then we simply add or subtract the numerators. For example:

$$\frac{3}{7}+\frac{5}{7}-\frac{2}{7}=\frac{(3+5-2)}{7}=\frac{6}{7}$$

$$\frac{4}{5}+\frac{3}{5}-\frac{1}{5}=\frac{(4+3-1)}{5}=1\tfrac{1}{5}$$

Where fractions that have to be added or subtracted do not have a common denominator, then you have to select a denominator which is common. The principle is that you select the lowest possible number into which all the denominators will divide, this is known as the *lowest common denominator*. You then convert the dissimilar fractions to that common denominator. For example:

In the problem $5/9 + 2/3 - 1/6$ the lowest common denominator of 9, 3 and 6 is 18. By converting all the fractions to a denominator of 18 we get:

$$\frac{10}{18}+\frac{12}{18}-\frac{3}{18}=\frac{(10+12-3)}{18}=\frac{19}{18} \quad \text{or} \quad 1\tfrac{1}{18}$$

Where you have whole numbers then you have to add (or subtract) them first and then add (or subtract) the fractions:

$$2\tfrac{7}{9}+3\tfrac{3}{4}-6\tfrac{1}{3}=2+3-6=-1+\frac{7}{9}+\frac{3}{4}-\frac{1}{3}$$

(the lowest common denominator of 9, 4 and 3 is 36)

$$= -1 + \frac{28 + 27 - 12}{36} = -1 + \frac{43}{36}$$

$$= -1 + 1\tfrac{7}{36} = \frac{7}{36}$$

The following example includes the principles which have been outlined in the chapter so far, and it illustrates what you should do when the total of fractions is negative.

$$4\tfrac{3}{7} - 1\tfrac{1}{2} - \frac{2}{3} = 3 + \frac{3}{7} - \frac{1}{2} - \frac{2}{3}$$

$$= 3 + \frac{18 - 21 - 28}{42}$$

$$= 3 + \left(-\frac{31}{42}\right)$$

The total of fractions is negative and therefore we have to put one of the whole numbers over the common denominator, and add it to the fraction:

$$= 2 + \frac{42}{42} - \frac{31}{42} = 2\tfrac{11}{42}$$

Exercise 2.3

(*a*) $\frac{7}{10} + \frac{1}{10} - \frac{6}{10}$ (*b*) $\frac{1}{15} + \frac{4}{5} - \frac{2}{3}$

(*c*) $\frac{3}{5} - \frac{7}{8} + \frac{1}{2} - \frac{1}{4} + \frac{5}{8}$ (*d*) $5\tfrac{7}{16} + 10\tfrac{5}{8} - 1\tfrac{1}{4}$

(*e*) $\frac{5}{7} + 3\tfrac{2}{3} + 5\tfrac{1}{2}$ (*f*) $7\tfrac{1}{12} + 2\tfrac{1}{6} - 4\tfrac{2}{5}$

(*g*) $1\tfrac{3}{11} - 4 - \left(3\tfrac{3}{4} + 6\tfrac{5}{6} - \frac{7}{12}\right)$ (*h*) $13\tfrac{7}{9} - \left(\frac{3}{4} - \frac{1}{2} - \frac{2}{5}\right)$

2.4 Multiplication of fractions

Before you start to multiply fractions you should convert any mixed numbers into improper fractions. For example $2\tfrac{1}{4}$ becomes $\tfrac{9}{4}$.

To multiply a fraction you first multiply the numerators, and then multiply the denominators to give a new fraction. For example:

$$2\tfrac{1}{4} \times 1\tfrac{3}{8} = \frac{9}{4} \times \frac{11}{8} = \frac{99}{32} = 3\tfrac{3}{32}$$

Very often a problem can be simplified by *cancelling*:

$$6\tfrac{1}{4} \times \frac{3}{7} \times 3\tfrac{1}{5} = \frac{\overset{5}{\cancel{25}}}{\underset{1}{\cancel{4}}} \times \frac{3}{7} \times \frac{\overset{4}{\cancel{16}}}{\underset{1}{\cancel{5}}}$$

5, 3 and 4 should now be multiplied to give the numerator; and then 1, 7 and 1 should be multiplied to give the denominator. This gives:

$$\frac{60}{7} = 8\tfrac{4}{7}$$

Exercise 2.4

(*a*) $\frac{3}{8} \times 4$ (*b*) $9\tfrac{1}{7} \times 2\tfrac{5}{8}$

(*c*) $\frac{6}{7}$ of $\frac{7}{12}$ (*d*) $\frac{5}{9} \times 2\tfrac{2}{35} \times 1\tfrac{5}{16}$

(*e*) $2\tfrac{2}{17} \times 1\tfrac{3}{5} \times 2\tfrac{11}{20}$ (*f*) $\frac{11}{56} \times 1\tfrac{15}{132}$ of 88

Note that *of* means the same as *times*, and when it occurs in a problem it should be replaced by the × sign.

2.5 Division of fractions

The method for dividing fractions is almost identical to the multiplication procedure. The rule is that an improper fraction which follows a division sign should be inverted, and the division sign is then replaced by a multiplication sign. For example:

$$5\tfrac{2}{5} \times 2\tfrac{6}{7} \div 4\tfrac{1}{2} = \frac{27}{5} \times \frac{20}{7} \div \frac{9}{2}$$

$$= \frac{27}{5} \times \frac{20}{7} \times \frac{2}{9}$$

$$= \frac{24}{7} = 3\tfrac{3}{7}$$

$$\frac{5}{8} \div \left(\frac{15}{14} \div \frac{40}{35}\right) = \frac{5}{8} \div \left(\frac{15}{14} \times \frac{35}{40}\right)$$

$$= \frac{5}{8} \div \frac{15}{16}$$

$$= \frac{5}{8} \times \frac{16}{15} = \frac{2}{3}$$

Alternatively,
$$= \frac{5}{8} \div \left(\frac{15}{14} \times \frac{35}{40}\right)$$
$$= \frac{5}{8} \times \frac{14}{15} \times \frac{40}{35} = \frac{2}{3}$$

Exercise 2.5

(*a*) $\frac{7}{32} \div 21$ (*b*) $1\frac{8}{11} \div 1\frac{13}{44}$

(*c*) $7\frac{4}{5} \div 1\frac{1}{25}$ (*d*) $\frac{16}{39} \times 2\frac{1}{6} \div 2\frac{2}{3}$

(*e*) $2\frac{1}{2}$ of $1\frac{3}{25} \div 1\frac{19}{30}$ (*f*) $(3\frac{1}{7} \div 6\frac{3}{5}) \times \frac{14}{25}$

(*g*) $2\frac{4}{7} \div (2\frac{10}{29} \times 5\frac{2}{17})$ (*h*) $\frac{4}{9} \div \left(1\frac{2}{3} \div \frac{15}{16}\right)$

2.6 Introduction to decimals

The function of decimals is similar to that of fractions; decimals represent parts or fractions of a whole number. The main aspect of a decimal number is the decimal point (.), which separates the whole number from the fraction.

The fraction part of a decimal has a denominator of 10 (or a multiple of 10), but the denominator is never shown. Thus

0.6 is the same as 6/10;
0.24 is the same as 24/100;
0.093 is the same as 93/1000.

A decimal fraction then, like a whole number, is expressed in units of ten, that is the number 582.356 is made up of:

Hundreds	*Tens*	*Units*	(.)	*Tenths*	*Hundredths*	*Thousandths*
5	8	2	.	3	5	6

2.7 Conversion of decimals to fractions

Examples:

$$0.35 = \frac{35}{100} = \frac{7}{20};$$
$$14.025 = 14\tfrac{25}{1000} = 14\tfrac{1}{40};$$
$$152.30 = 152\tfrac{30}{100} = 152\tfrac{3}{10}.$$

You can see from the three examples that the number of digits after the decimal point determine the denominator:

one digit after the decimal point has a denominator of 10
two digits after the decimal point have a denominator of 100
three digits after the decimal point have a denominator of 1000
and so on.

You can add any number of 0s to the end of a decimal fraction and this will not affect its value. Thus: 0.2 is the same as 0.20 or 0.200 or 0.2000 or 0.200000.

Exercise 2.7

Convert the following decimals to fractions:

(*a*) 4.2	(*b*) 56.89	(*c*) 150.036
(*d*) 0.007	(*e*) 706.900	(*f*) 0.105
(*g*) 0.45	(*h*) 10.1010	(*i*) 369.419

2.8 Conversion of fractions to decimals

Examples:

$$\frac{4}{5} = \frac{4.0}{5} = 0.8$$

$$\frac{1}{16} = \frac{1.0000}{16} = 0.0625$$

$$9\tfrac{1}{16} = 9\frac{1.0000}{16} = 9.0625$$

You will see from these three examples that in order to convert fractions to decimals the numerator is divided by the denominator. 0s are added to the numerator until the division is complete.

However, in many instances, even though 0s are added the division cannot be completed. For example, in the conversion of $\frac{2}{3}$ to a decimal number we get 0.6666 and the division can never be completed; the 6 keeps on recurring. In these instances the decimal number is *rounded* to the required number of decimal places; this depends on the degree of accuracy required in the answer.

2.9 Approximation

A number with one digit after the decimal point is said to be correct to one decimal place; a number with two digits after the decimal point is correct to two decimal places, and so on.

In order to reduce a number to the required number of decimal places we have to *round up* or *round down*. Having determined the number of decimal places, if the next digit, after the last decimal place, is 5 or more, then you should round up. Conversely if it is less than 5 you should round down. For example:

6.2315 correct to one decimal place is 6.2
0.035 correct to two decimal places is 0.04
9.9847 correct to three decimal places is 9.985

Exercise 2.9

Convert the following fractions to decimals:

(*a*) $\frac{3}{8}$ (*b*) $\frac{7}{25}$ (*c*) $\frac{5}{16}$ (*d*) $\frac{17}{20}$

(*e*) $\frac{3}{7}$ (correct to 2 d.p.) (*f*) $\frac{13}{16}$ (correct to 3 d.p.)

(*g*) $\frac{5}{6}$ (correct to 4 d.p.) (*h*) $\frac{3}{410}$ (correct to 2 d.p.)

2.10 Addition and subtraction of decimals

Since a decimal number is like a whole number, in that it is made up of units of 10, then the addition and subtraction of decimals is almost exactly the same as the addition and subtraction of whole numbers.

The only difference is in the decimal point. When you are working with decimals try to ensure that the decimal points are aligned so that you are only adding and subtracting the appropriate units. Consider the following examples:

(*a*) Add the following; 45.83, 789.01, 56 947, 0.003 and 2.407

	45.830
	789.010
	56 947.000
	0.003
	2.407
Answer	57 784.250

(*b*) Subtract 71 600.89 from 851 933.558

	851 933.558
	71 600.890
Answer	780 332.668

(*c*) Calculate 29.31 + 456.027 − 65.99 + 300.06 − 5126 − 785.2144

Positive numbers	*Negative numbers*
29.310	65.9900
456.027	5126.0000
300.060	785.2144
+ 785.397	− 5977.2044

$$\begin{array}{r} +\ 785.3970 \\ -\ 5977.2044 \\ \hline -\ 5191.8074 \end{array}$$

Answer − 5191.8074

Exercise 2.10

(*a*) 5984.2 + 2316 − 0.005 − 36.2004 + 1200.26 − 0.08
(*b*) 0.0005 − 236.981 − 22.1 + 13 + 0.09 − 589.4755
(*c*) − 22.66 + 5.0908 + 89547.3 + 13.25 − 567 − 0.007
(*d*) 0.2 + 996.003 − 56.147 + (− 38 + 12 564.89) + 22.4 658
(*e*) 4.06 − (− 22.6035 − 600.88) − 51.7 + 998 + 0.031

2.11 Multiplication and division of decimals

When decimal numbers are multiplied by 10 then the decimal point moves back one place, when multiplied by 100 it moves two places, 1000 three places, and so on. For example:

$$128.06 \times 10 = 1280.6$$

Similarly when a decimal number is divided by 10 then the decimal point moves forward one place, when divided by 100 it moves two places, 1000 three places, and so on. For example:

$$90.658 \div 1000 = 0.090658$$

When decimals are multiplied by any other numbers then you should add the number of digits after the decimal point in the question and this gives the number of decimal places in the answer. For example:

$$32.4 \times 7.659 = 248.1516$$

In the example given above since the left-hand side of the equation has a total of four digits after the decimal point, then the right-hand side (the answer) must also have four decimal places.

A numeracy skill which is particularly useful when dealing with decimals is to estimate the answer before working it out in detail. So an approximation of the problem given above;

$$32.4 \times 7.659$$

is $32 \times 8 = 256$

We know from this approximate answer where the decimal point should be, and the correct answer is 248.1516.

When decimals are divided by numbers other than 10, 100, etc., then, if it is necessary, you should move the decimal point the same number of places both in the numerator and the denominator so that the denominator becomes a whole number. Consider the following examples:

$$\frac{23.634}{4.68} = \frac{2363.4}{468} = 5.05$$

$$\frac{73.7}{0.055} = \frac{73700}{55} = 1340$$

Exercise 2.11

Simplify the following correct to 3 decimal places:

(*a*) 59.03×12.6 (*b*) 0.667×487 (*c*) 0.005×0.0099
(*d*) $21 \div 5.22$ (*e*) $470.26 \div 10.347$ (*f*) $0.0074 \div 2.56$
(*g*) $77.04 \times 0.06 \div 14.23$
(*h*) $(0.25 \div 0.009) \div 785.2$
(*i*) $16(2.88 \div 741.56)$
(*j*) $(77.56 \div 0.02) \div (6699 \times 1.0006)$

Worked examples

1 A firm produces five different types of lawn seed, A, B, C, D and E, and its production figures for a one-week period are: A = 900 kg, B = 1125 kg, C = 225 kg, D = 1800 kg, E = 450 kg.
(a) Express the weekly production figures for types of seed in fractions of the total production.
(b) If the production of type B decreased by 675 kg, and the production of type D increased by 450 kg, what difference would this make to total production and to the fractions of type B and type D?
(c) If the production of type A decreased by $\frac{1}{3}$, and type C increased by $\frac{1}{9}$, what difference would this make to total production and to the fractions of type A and type C?

Answer
(a) Total production = 4500 kg;

$\therefore$ type A = 900/4500 = 9/45 = 1/5;
type B = 1125/4500 = 225/900 = 1/4;
type C = 225/4500 = 45/900 = 5/100 = 1/20;
type D = 1800/4500 = 18/45 = 2/5;
type E = 450/4500 = 45/450 = 1/10.

(b) Total production = 4500 − 675 + 450 = 4275 kg;
∴ type B = 450/4275 = 90/855 = 18/171 = 2/19;
type D = 2250/4275 = 450/855 = 90/171 = 10/19.

(c) Reduction in type A = 900 × 1/3 = 300 kg;
Increase in type C = 225 × 1/9 = 25 kg;
∴ Total production = 4500 − 300 + 25 = 4225 kg.
∴ type A = 600/4225 = 120/845 = 24/169;
type C = 250/4225 = 50/845 = 10/169.

2
(a) Convert the answers in part (a) of question **1** to decimals.
(b) Convert the answers in part (b) of question **1** to decimals correct to three decimal places.
(c) Convert the answers in part (c) of question **1** to decimals correct to two decimal places.

Answer
(a) A = 1/5 = 0.2; B = 1/4 = 0.25; C = 1/20 = 0.05
D = 2/5 = 0.4; E = 1/10 = 0.1.

(b) type B = 2/19 = 0.105 correct to three decimal places
type D = 10/19 = 0.526 correct to three decimal places

(c) type A = 24/169 = 0.14 correct to two decimal places
type C = 10/169 = 0.06 correct to two decimal places

3 A garage has 13 employees who are paid at the following weekly rates:

		£ per week
1	foreman	185.24
7	mechanics	109.96
2	apprentices	75.55
3	clerk/receptionists	82.34

(a) Calculate the total weekly wage bill.
(b) If the weekly rate for the apprentices increases by 3/19, how much less money than a mechanic will an apprentice receive each week?
(c) If for each week that is worked the employer puts an additional 1/21 on one side for holiday pay, how much holiday pay will the foreman receive after 48 working weeks?

Answer
(a) £185.24 + £109.96 × 7 + £75.55 × 2 + £82.34 × 3
= £185.24 + £769.72 + £151.10 + £247.02
= £1353.08

(b) New weekly rate $= £75.55 + (£75.55 \times 3/19)$
$= £75.55 + £11.93 = £87.48$

Difference between mechanics and apprentices is

$$£109.96 - £87.48 = £22.48$$

(c) The foreman will receive

$$48 \times (£185.24 \times \tfrac{1}{21}) = 48 \times £8.82 = £423.36$$

Additional exercises

1 A firm produces different blends of tea, A, B, C and D, and the annual sales of the four blends are:

blend A	30 tons
blend B	40 tons
blend C	50 tons
blend D	60 tons

(a) Express the sales for each blend as fractions of total sales.
(b) If, in the following year, the sales of blend B increased by $\frac{1}{15}$, how many tons of blend B would have been sold?
(c) If the sales of blend A decreased by $\frac{1}{3}$ and blend C increased by $\frac{3}{5}$ what difference would this make to total sales and to the fractions of sales of blends A and C?

2 A pharmaceutical firm produces an indigestion mixture which contains the following in each 0.5 litre:

magnesium carbonate	22.3 gm
sodium bicarbonate	15.0 gm
calcium carbonate	27.5 gm

The average weekly production is 44 litres.

(a) How many grams of magnesium carbonate are used each week?
(b) How many weeks will a batch of sodium bicarbonate last if each batch weighs 121 kg?
(c) Calculate the weekly increase in the cost of calcium carbonate if its price increases from £13.25 per kg to £17.50 per kg.

3 Employees engaged in the assembly of radios are paid 75 p for each radio which they assemble plus the following daily bonuses:

Employee's daily output of radios	*Additional bonus for each radio £*
0–24	0
25–32	1/8 × 75p
33–40	1/4 × 75p
41–44	3/8 × 75p
45 or more	9/16 × 75p

Thus if an employee assembled 37 radios in one day she would receive:

Bonus pay	24×0	= £00.00
	$8 \times \frac{1}{8} \times 75$p	= £00.75
	$5 \times \frac{1}{4} \times 75$p	= £00.94
Basic pay	37×75p	= £27.75
Total pay for the day		= £29.44

(a) Calculate the earnings of an employee who assembled 48 radios in one day.
(b) How many radios would an employee have to assemble in a day to earn £28.50?
(c) Assuming that all employees work a five-day week, if the average daily number of radios assembled by each employee is 33, calculate the average weekly earnings.

4 There are five partners in a firm of solicitors, and they have agreed to share any profits in the following way:

Partner	A	3/35
Partner	B	1/7
Partner	C	1/5
Partner	D	9/35
Partner	E	11/35

(a) Express each partner's share in the profits in decimal numbers correct to 4 decimal places.
(b) If, in one year, the total profits of the firm amounted to £49 000, calculate how much partner D received.
(c) If, in one year, partners A and C received a combined total of £24 000, calculate how much partner E received.
(d) Partner B resigned from the firm in a year when the total profits were £52 500. B had worked for the firm for just two months of the year and received 1/6 of his annual share. Calculate how much partner B received.

5 A manufacturer of steel plate has supplied the following quantities to a customer:

Quantity	*Length*	*Width*	*Thickness* (*inches*)
6 *plates*	$6\frac{3}{8}$	$4\frac{1}{4}$	$\frac{1}{16}$
16 *plates*	$7\frac{3}{16}$	$5\frac{5}{8}$	$\frac{1}{4}$
21 plates	$14\frac{7}{16}$	$9\frac{3}{32}$	$\frac{1}{2}$

(a) Express the length and width of the $\frac{1}{16}''$ plate in metric units. ($1'' = 2.4$ cm).
(b) Calculate, in imperial units, the total area of the $\frac{1}{4}''$ plate supplied (area of a plate is one face).
(c) Calculate, in metric units, the total volume of $\frac{1}{2}''$ plate supplied.

3 Percentages and ratios

3.1 Introduction to percentages

A percentage is a fraction; the word *percent* means per hundred, and all percentages are fractions of 100. We normally write percent as % which simply means /100. For example:

$$17\% \text{ means } 17 \text{ in every } 100 \text{ or } \frac{17}{100}$$

$$33\tfrac{1}{3}\% \text{ means } 33\tfrac{1}{3} \text{ in every } 100 \text{ or } \frac{33\frac{1}{3}}{100}, \text{ i.e. } \tfrac{1}{3}$$

$$100\% \text{ means } 100 \text{ in every } 100 \text{ or } \frac{100}{100}, \text{ i.e. } 1$$

So if unemployment stands at 10% then $\frac{1}{10}$ of the working population, or 10 workers in every 100, are registered as unemployed.

3.2 Converting percentages to fractions

We can see from the examples given above that in order to convert a percentage to a fraction we divide the percentage by 100. Thus $72\% = \frac{72}{100} = \frac{18}{25}$.

Exercise 3.2

Convert the following percentages to fractions:

(*a*) 75%	(*b*) 30%	(*c*) 82%
(*d*) 45%	(*e*) 6%	(*f*) 92%
(*g*) $12\frac{1}{2}\%$	(*h*) $66\frac{2}{3}\%$	(*i*) $56\frac{1}{2}\%$

3.3 Converting fractions to percentages

Since all percentage figures are fractions of 100 they provide a useful measure for comparing all kinds of statistics such as prices, wages, profitability, and so on. Consequently, it is often useful to show simple fractions as percentages, and in order to do this we multiply the fraction by 100%. For example:

$$\frac{4}{5} = \frac{4}{5} \times \frac{100}{1}\% = \frac{400}{5}\% = 80\%$$

$$2\tfrac{3}{4} = \frac{11}{4} \times \frac{100}{1}\% = \frac{1100}{4}\% = 275\%$$

$$\frac{3}{16} = \frac{3}{16} \times \frac{100}{1}\% = \frac{300}{16}\% = 18\tfrac{3}{4}\%$$

Exercise 3.3

Convert the following fractions to percentages:

(*a*) $\frac{1}{8}$ (*b*) $\frac{3}{15}$ (*c*) $\frac{17}{1000}$

(*d*) $\frac{7}{12}$ (*e*) $\frac{19}{25}$ (*f*) $\frac{6}{75}$

(*g*) $\frac{142}{213}$ (*h*) $\frac{484}{222}$ (*i*) $\frac{563}{154}$

3.4 Finding a percentage of a given quantity

In order to calculate a percentage of a given quantity it is useful to remember that:

(1) % can be expressed as /100;
(2) 'of' can be replaced by × (times).

Thus:

32% of £4162
= £32/100 × 4162/1
= £1331.84

Exercise 3.4

Find (*a*) 60% of 42 (*b*) 45% of £360
(*c*) $22\tfrac{1}{2}$% of 5160 km (*d*) 5% of 447 litres

3.5 Expressing one number or quantity as a percentage of another

In order to express one number as a percentage of another the number is first expressed as a fraction of the other number and then converted to a percentage by multiplying by 100 %. For example:

Express 3.4 km as a percentage of 15 km.

Answer $\frac{3.4}{15} \times \frac{100}{1\%} = 22.67\%$

Exercise 3.5

(*a*) What percentage of 50 is 5?
(*b*) What percentage of 1020 is 17?
(*c*) Express £13 as a percentage of £65?
(*d*) Express 5.2 km as a percentage of 72 km?

3.6 Calculating the 'whole', i.e. 100 %, from a given percentage

The method for calculating 100 % from a given percentage is illustrated by the following example:

Find the total amount if 36.4 is equal to 14 %.

Answer $14\% = 36.4 \therefore 1\% = \frac{36.4}{14}$

$\therefore 100\% = \frac{36.4}{14} \times 100 = 260$

Exercise 3.6

(*a*) Find the total quantity of which 4 gram is 20 %.
(*b*) What is the total amount if 11 % equals 56.43?
(*c*) If 137.7 cm is $67\frac{1}{2}\%$ what is the total amount?
(*d*) Find the 'whole' given that 70 % is £101.50.

3.7 Calculating a percentage change

If the quantity or the value of an item increases or decreases it is often more useful in business to express the increase or decrease as a percentage of the original. This is illustrated in the following two examples.

Example 3.7a

The number of people employed in the accounts section of a large organisation increased during one year from 150 to 180 employees.

Find the percentage increase in the number of employees.

Answer Actual increase = 180 − 150 = 30 employees
Original number of employees = 150 employees

$$\text{Percentage increase} = \frac{30}{150} \times 100\% = 20\%$$

Example 3.7b

The price of a bicycle was reduced in a sale from £89 to £76.50. Find the percentage decrease in the price.

Answer Actual decrease = £89.00 − £76.50 = £12.50
Original price = £89.00
Percentage decrease = 12.50/89 × 100%
= 14.04%

Exercise 3.7

(*a*) Decrease 350 by 8% and by 26%.
(*b*) Increase 125 by 12% and by 32%.
(*c*) Decrease 56 by 5% and by 60%.
(*d*) Increase 48 by 18% and by $12\frac{1}{2}$%.

3.8 Ratios

Ratios are like percentages in that they are a convenient method for comparing similar quantities. They are often used in the analysis of business statistics, particularly in financial analysis and the analysis of production figures.

For example, if a company's gross profit is £36 000 and the sales are £216 000 we can compare these two variables by saying that the gross profit is 36 000/216 000 of sales. Alternatively we could say that the ratio of gross profit to sales is 36 000 to 216 000.

The ratio 36 000 to 216 000 is usually written 36 000:216 000. Ratios are like fractions in that, where possible, they should be reduced to their simplest form. Thus 36 000:216 000 can be reduced to 1:6. From this ratio we know that gross profit is $\frac{1}{6}$ of sales and that the ratio of sales to profit is 6:1, i.e. sales are six times greater than gross profit.

We may want to compare the profit ratio of one company with the profit ratio of a similar company. In order to do this the ratio is expressed in the form of n:1 so that, using the example given above, the profit ratio of 1:6 becomes 0.167:1.

Example 3.8a

The following shows the sales and gross profit for the same period of two shirt manufacturers:

	Sales (£)	*Gross profit* (£)
Company A	420 000	37 350
Company B	627 000	51 500

Which company has the higher profit ratio?

Answer

Company A profit : sales = 37 350 : 420 000 = 0.089 : 1
Company B profit : sales = 51 500 : 627 000 = 0.082 : 1
Company A has the higher profit ratio.

It is important to remember that ratios can be used only to compare quantities which are similar; for instance distance cannot be compared with weight. Equally ratios are valid only when the variables are expressed in the same units. So in a problem that includes $ and £, any values shown in a ratio must be converted to a common currency.

Example 3.8b

If the maximum speed of the British Advanced Passenger Train (APT) is 120 miles per hour and the maximum speed of the French APT is 209 km per hour, express the two speeds in the form of a ratio.

Answer 1 km = 0.6214 mile

$\therefore$ 209 km × 0.6214 miles/km = 130 miles

The ratio of the speed of the British APT to the French APT is 120 : 130 = 12 : 13.

Ratios can include more than two quantities, and when this occurs the ratio gives us a variety of comparisons. For example, a paint manufacturer, in order to produce a particular colour of green, mixes 80 litres of yellow paint, 100 litres of blue, and 20 litres of white. The ratio of yellow to blue to white is 80 : 100 : 20 = 4 : 5 : 1. These three may be expressed as ratios of one another. For example:

yellow : blue = 4 : 5
yellow : white = 4 : 1
blue : white = 5 : 1

Example 3.8c

The constituents of an alloy produced by a metal manufacturer are:

copper	48 parts
zinc	16 parts
tin	4 parts

If the copper costs five times as much per part as both zinc and tin, and the manufacturer spends £1200 a week on copper how much is spent on zinc and tin each week?

Answer
Copper costs £1200 a week and this represents 48 parts.
∴ 16 parts = £400 and 4 parts = £100.
∴ the amount spent on zinc = £400/5 = £80;
and the amount spent on tin = £100/5 = £20.

Exercise 3.8

(*a*) By expressing the following ratios in the form of $n:1$ calculate which is the greater of each pair:
(i) 6:4 and 8:5 (ii) 14 kg:11 kg and 41 kg:32 kg (iii) $\frac{1}{2}:\frac{1}{6}$ and $\frac{1}{3}:\frac{1}{8}$
(*b*) The capital contributed by three partners is:

A = £35 000
B = £45 000
C = £80 000

If the profits of the partnership are to be shared in the proportion of the capital contributed calculate how much each partner would receive if the profits were £27 500.
(*c*) A person's gross income in a year is £8420 from which £2105 is deducted for taxation. What is the ratio of tax paid for each £ earned?

Worked examples

1 A firm employs 450 people of whom 270 are female, and 22 of the males are registered as disabled.
(a) What percentage of the employees are male?
(b) What percentage of the males are disabled?

Answer
(a) The number of males employed = 450 − 270 = 180

$$\therefore \text{ the percentage of males } = \frac{180}{450} \times \frac{100}{1}\% = \frac{18000}{450}\% = 40\%$$

(b) The percentage of the males who are disabled is

$$\frac{22}{180} \times \frac{100}{1\%} = \frac{2200}{180\%} = 12.2\%$$

2 An insurance company pays everyone on its salesforce a basic salary of £5000 per annum, plus 3% of the annual premiums paid by each sales person's clients. However when the sum of such premiums exceeds £200 000 then the company pays 5% on the excess, and this percentage is increased by $\frac{1}{2}$% for every extra £20 000, which the company receives.

The following shows the premiums paid in one year by the clients of three members of the company's salesforce:

(a)	Salesperson X	£192 563
(b)	Salesperson Y	£206 388
(c)	Salesperson Z	£223 110

Calculate their earnings for that year.

Answer

(a) X's basic pay = £5000

$$\text{bonus pay} = 3\% \text{ of } £192\,563 = \frac{3}{100} \times \frac{£192\,563}{1}$$

$$= £5776.89$$

Total pay = £5000 + £5776.89 = £10 776.89

(b) Y's basic pay = £5000

$$\text{bonus pay} = 3\% \text{ of } £200\,000 = \frac{3}{100} \times \frac{£200\,000}{1}$$

$$= £6000$$

$$+\,5\% \text{ of } £6388 = \frac{5}{100} \times \frac{£6388}{1}$$

$$= £319.40$$

Total pay = £5000 + £6000 + £319.40 = £11 319.40

(c) Z's basic pay = £5000

$$\text{bonus pay} = 3\% \text{ of } £200\,000 = \frac{3}{100} \times \frac{£200\,000}{1}$$

$$= £6000$$

$$+\,5\% \text{ of } £20\,000 = \frac{5}{100} \times \frac{£20\,000}{1}$$

$$= £1000$$

$$+\,5\tfrac{1}{2}\% \text{ of } £3110 = \frac{11}{200} \times £3110$$

$$= £171.05$$

Total pay = £5000 + £6000 + £1000 + £171.05 = £12 171.05

3 The following details have been extracted from the Profit and Loss Account of a retail shop:

Sales	£107 236
Expenses	£ 91 021
Profit	£ 16 215

(a) Express the expenses as a percentage of sales.
(b) If the profits were taxed at a rate of 35% how much tax would the owner of the shop have to pay?
(c) If, in the following year, the profits of the shop increased by 11% what were the profits for that year?

Answer
(a) Sometimes, when we are comparing large financial sums, it is acceptable to round the figures, providing of course that such rounding does not distort the comparison. So, in this case, expenses expressed as a percentage of sales are:

$$\frac{91}{107} \times \frac{100}{1\%} = 85\%$$

(b) The owner would have to pay:

$$35\% \text{ of } £16\,215 = \frac{35}{100} \times £16\,215 = £5\,675.25$$

(c) The profits for the year are 111% of £16 215

$$= \frac{111}{100} \times £16\,215 = £17\,998.65$$

4 A mail order firm has notified its customers of reductions in the price of the following goods:

(a) An electric kettle – sale price £11.90 – a reduction of 15%.
(b) A pine bed reduced by £56.42 – a reduction of 20%.
(c) A lawnmower originally £67.50 – sale price £54.00.
Calculate the original price of the kettle and the bed, and the percentage reduction in the price of the lawnmower.

Answer
(a) Sale price of the kettle is 85% of the original price,

i.e. $\frac{85}{100} \times \text{original price} = £11.90$;

$\therefore$ original price $= \frac{100}{85} \times £11.90 = £14.00$.

(b) Since 20% is equivalent to £56.42,

then 1% is equivalent to $\frac{£56.42}{20} = £2.8210$;

$\therefore$ the original price of the bed is $100 \times £2.8210 = £282.10$.

(c) The mower is reduced by £13.50 which expressed as a percentage of the original price is:

$$\frac{13.50}{67.50} \times \frac{100}{1\%} = 20\%$$

5 A partnership has three partners, A, B and C, and the profits are divided in the ratio A : B : C = 8 : 4 : 2. At the end of a financial year the interest paid out of the Profit and Loss Account is £2450 which is 7% of the total profit. The remaining profit is divided in the ratio given above.

(a) Calculate the total profit.
(b) How much profit did each partner receive?
(c) What percentage of the total profit did Partner B receive?

Answer

(a) Total profit = 100%

$$7\% \text{ of the total profit} = £2450$$

$$\therefore 100\% = \frac{£2450}{7} \times 100$$

$$\therefore \text{total profit} = £35\,000$$

(b) The amount divided between the partners is

$$£35\,000 - £2\,450 = £32\,550$$

Partner A received $\frac{8}{14} \times £32\,550 = £18\,600$

Partner B received $\frac{4}{14} \times £32\,550 = £\ 9\,300$

Partner C received $\frac{2}{14} \times £32\,550 = £\ 4\,650$

(c) Total profit = £35 000
Partner B received £9 300

$$\therefore \text{B's \% share of total profit} = \frac{9\,300}{35\,000} \times 100\% = 26.57\%$$

6 Four firms, A, B, C and D, have negotiated a joint contract on the use of a mainframe computer under which they are charged a flat rate of £120 per six-hour period regardless of the time spent using the computer – the computer can be used by all four firms at any one time. The firms agree that the cost of £120 will be shared in proportion to the time each spends using the computer. The usage for one six-hour period is:

Time	*Users*
9.00 – 10.00	A B D
10.00 – 11.00	B D
11.00 – 12.00	A B C D
12.00 – 1.00	A B
1.00 – 2.00	B C D
2.00 – 3.00	B

If an additional premium of £2 is charged each time a user is connected to the computer how much should each firm pay for the six-hour period.

Answer
The total number of hours used by each firm is:
A = 3 hours; B = 6 hours; C = 2 hours; D = 4 hours
∴ the £120 cost should be shared in the ratio:

A:B:C:D = 3:6:2:4

A's share is £3/15 × 120 = £24
B's share is £6/15 × 120 = £48
C's share is £2/15 × 120 = £16
D's share is £4/15 × 120 = £32

A is connected twice at 9.00 and at 11.00
∴ A's additional premium is £4 making a total cost of £28.
B's premium is £2 and total cost £50
C's premium is £4 and total cost £20
D's premium is £4 and total cost £36

Additional exercises

1 The following table shows the employment of full-time teaching staff at universities in Great Britain:

	1964/5	*1974/5*
Professors	2175	3987
Readers	3508	7661
Lecturers	10266	23285
Others	1168	2017

(a) Calculate the percentage increase in each category.
(b) Express each category as a percentage of the total employed in each academic year. Show your answer in tabular form.

2 The following table shows the percentage growth in population in 50 years from 1911 of 4 English cities:

	1911	*% increase by 1961*
Liverpool	113000	560
Leeds	164000	212
Sheffield	184000	168
Wolverhampton	69000	119

(a) Using the information calculate the actual 1961 population figures for each of the 4 cities.
(b) In 1971 the population of Wolverhampton was 269000. Express the 1971 figure as a percentage of the 1911 population.

(c) In 1971 the population of Liverpool was 610 000. Calculate the percentage change from 1961 to 1971.

3 Two estate agents have the following scale of fees:

Agent X		*Agent Y*	
Selling price (£)	(%)	*Selling price (£)*	(%)
on the first £20 000	$2\frac{1}{2}$	on the first £15 000	2
on the next £25 000	1	on the next £15 000	$1\frac{1}{2}$
on the remainder	$\frac{1}{2}$	on the next £20 000	1
		on the remainder	$\frac{1}{2}$

(a) Construct a chart to compare the graduated fee structure of the two agents.
(b) Calculate the fees charged by both agents on the following selling prices: £29 250, £36 900, £42 500, and use the chart to verify your answer.

4 A small builder purchases a van and lorry for £2450 and £5320 respectively. The depreciation charge on these two assets is a fixed percentage which is charged on an annual basis. If the depreciation rate on the van is $33\frac{1}{3}$ % and on the lorry is 25 % calculate the value of both vehicles after four years.

5 A bankrupt owes three creditors £425, £695 and £720. His total assets are £840. How much should the biggest creditor receive?

6 The following shows the index of retail prices for four consecutive years:

year 1	119.4
year 2	125.0
year 3	131.8
year 4	140.2

(a) If the weekly expenses of a family in year 1 were £42.30 what would you estimate the weekly expenses of a family with a similar expenditure to have been in year 4?
(b) If the index of retail prices for year 2 was changed to represent 100.0 show the index for each of the other three years.

4 Equations

4.1 Introduction

This chapter shows how simple equations can be solved, and illustrates how such solutions are used in business. Complex equations will not be used; we shall concentrate on elementary examples of practical equations.

In some instances established formulae are used to demonstrate the nature and application of equations. It is assumed that the validity of such formulae will be accepted since their derivation is beyond the scope of the text.

Equations deal with relationships, and so an equation includes variables which are often represented by x, y and z. Sometimes an equation can also include a constant which stands for any given number. A *constant*, as the term implies, has a fixed value; whereas a *variable* varies in relation to the other variables in the equation.

A simple example of an equation is the conversion of one variable to another such as the conversion of centigrade into fahrenheit:

$$\text{Given the equation } F = \tfrac{9}{5} \times C + 32$$

(where the variable F = degrees fahrenheit, the variable C = degrees centigrade, and 32 is the constant),
then, for any given value of C, the value of F can be calculated. Thus:

$$\text{when } C = 10 \text{ degrees, } F = \frac{9}{5} \times 10 + 32 = 50.0 \text{ degrees}$$

$$\text{when } C = 38 \text{ degrees, } F = \frac{9}{5} \times 38 + 32 = 100.4 \text{ degrees}$$

Many equations deal with relationships that include powers and roots. Sections 4.2 to 4.5 briefly revise the principles of calculation of powers and roots.

4.2 Powers

When a number is multiplied by itself several times the expression can be abbreviated by using index notation. For example,

the expression $z \times z \times z \times z = z^4$

z^4 is z to the power of 4

z is the base number and ^{4} is the index

The following simple example shows the value of 5 to various powers:

$5^1 = 5$	five to the power of one
$5^2 = 5 \times 5 = 25$	five squared
$5^3 = 5 \times 5 \times 5 = 125$	five cubed
$5^4 = 5 \times 5 \times 5 \times 5 = 625$	five to the power of four
$5^n = \underbrace{5 \times 5 \times 5. . . \times 5}_{\text{n terms}}$	five to the power n

n.b. Any number to the power 0 equals 1. Thus:

$$5^\circ = 1$$
$$\tfrac{3}{4}^\circ = 1$$
$$10\,000^\circ = 1$$

4.3 Negative indices

Where we have a negative power the expression can be written as a denominator of a fraction and the negative sign becomes positive. Thus:

$$x^{-a} = \frac{1}{x^a}$$

For example:

$$4^{-3} = \frac{1}{4^3} = \frac{1}{64}$$

Exercise 4.3

Evaluate the following:

(*a*) 13^2	(*b*) 6^3	(*c*) 17^0	(*d*) 27^{-1}
(*e*) $4^2 \times 6^{-1}$	(*f*) $2^4 \times 5^2$	(*g*) $2^3 \times 7^2 \times 3^2$	(*h*) $4^3 \times 5^0 \times 7^1$
(*i*) $8^3 \div 2^{-4}$	(*j*) $7^3 \div 5^1$	(*k*) $4^2 \times 3^3 \div 2^4$	(l) $7^2 \times 4^2 \div 10^0$

4.4 Roots

Calculating the square root of a given number is the reverse process of calculating the square. For example:

Since $5^2 = 25$ then the square root of 25 $(\sqrt{25}) = 5$
Similarly since $4^3 = 64$ then $\sqrt[3]{64} = 4$

An alternative method of writing a root sign such as $\sqrt[n]{x}$ is to express it as a fractional index $x^{\frac{1}{n}}$. Thus:

$\sqrt[3]{125}$ is the cube root of 125 which can also be written $125^{\frac{1}{3}}$ and $\sqrt[4]{16}$ is the fourth root of 16 which can be written $16^{\frac{1}{4}}$

Exercise 4.4

Evaluate the following:

(*a*) $\sqrt{169}$	(*b*) $\sqrt[4]{16}$	(*c*) $\sqrt[3]{64}$	(*d*) $49^{\frac{1}{2}}$
(*e*) $8^{\frac{1}{3}}$	(*f*) $625^{\frac{1}{4}}$	(*g*) $36^{-\frac{1}{2}}$	(*h*) $14\,641^{-\frac{1}{4}}$

4.5 Index laws

In order to multiply powers which have the same base the indices are added. Thus:

$$a^3 \times a^2 = a^{(3+2)} = a^5$$

The validity of this law can be checked very easily by the following example:

$$a^3 \times a^2 = a \times a \times a \times a \times a = a^5$$

To divide powers which have the same base the indices are subtracted. Thus:

$$b^4 \div b^1 = b^{(4-1)} = b^3$$

The validity of this law is illustrated by the following example:

$$b^4 \div b^1 = \frac{\not{b} \times b \times b \times b}{\not{b}} = b^3$$

To find the power of a power the indices are multiplied. Thus,

$$(c^4)^3 = c^{4 \times 3} = c^{12}.$$

Another way of looking at this is

$$(c^4)^3 = c^4 \times c^4 \times c^4 = c^{4+4+4} = c^{12}$$

These three index laws can be summarised as follows:

$$y^a \times y^b = y^{a+b}$$
$$y^a \div y^b = y^{a-b}$$
$$(y^a)^b = y^{ab}$$

Exercise 4.5

Simplify the following:

(*a*) $y^2 \times y^5$	(*b*) $y^6 \div y^1$	(*c*) $(y^2)^3$	(*d*) $y^2 \times y^{-2}$
(*e*) $(y^3)^{\frac{1}{3}}$	(*f*) $y^{\frac{1}{2}} - y^{\frac{1}{3}}$	(*g*) $(y^{\frac{1}{2}})^{-2} \times (y^{\frac{1}{3}})^{\frac{1}{2}} \times (y^{-5})^{-1}$	

(*h*) $(y^{\frac{1}{3}})^6 \times y' - (y^{-4})^2$

4.6 Solving simple equations

If we have a simple equation which has one unknown value then that equation can be rearranged to find that value. The general rule is that whatever is done to one side of the equation must be done to the other side of that equation. For example:

Find the value of y when $\sqrt{\dfrac{3y+6}{2}} = 3$

Step 1 Remove the square root by squaring both sides:

$$\frac{3y+6}{2} = 9$$

Step 2 Remove the denominator 2 by multiplying both sides by 2:

$$3y+6 = 18$$

Step 3 Remove the 6 by substracting 6 from each side:

$$3y = 12$$

Step 4 Remove the 3 by dividing both sides by 3:

$$y = 4$$

n.b. In the above example there is only one possible value for y. However, when equations include variables that are raised to a power this means that there is more than one possible solution for the value of the variable.

4.7 Rearrangement of a formula

In equations where there are two variables the method of rearrangement can be used to express one variable in terms of the other. For example, the temperature conversion formula: $F = \frac{9}{5} \times C + 32$ has two variables F and C, and this equation can be rearranged so that C is expressed in terms of F:

Step 1 Multiply each side by 5:

$$5F = 9C + 32 \times 5$$

Step 2 Subtract 32×5 from each side:

$$5F - (32 \times 5) = 9C$$

This can be written as:

$$5 \times (F - 32) = 9C$$

Step 3 Divide each side by 9:

$$\tfrac{5}{9} \times (F - 32) = C$$

We can now use this equation to find any value of C given the value of F. So when $F = 59$ degrees then

$$C = \tfrac{5}{9} \times (27)$$

$$C = 15 \text{ degrees}$$

In this simple example we have shown that an equation can be rearranged so that it can be expressed in terms of either variable.

4.8 Substituting values into formulae

In order to solve some business problems formulae have been derived which show the relationship between variables in a simple equation. For instance, accountants have devised a method for discounting future money values into present day money values by applying an equation known as the *Net Present Value formula*:

$$NPV = \left[\frac{i}{(1+c)^n}\right] - o$$

where NPV = Net Present Value
i = inflow of cash
o = outflow of cash
c = cost of finance
n = number of years of projected values

By substituting known values into the formula the Net Present Value of future projects can be determined. For example, a company's directors are given estimated costs and returns for two similar investment projects. It is estimated that one project would take five years to complete but the other only three years. The directors want to compare the estimated costs and returns in current money values. By substituting the known and the anticipated values into the NPV formula the two projects can be expressed in present day terms and a realistic comparison can be made.

The information which the directors had was:

	Project A	*Project B*
Cash outflow	£40 000	£50 000
Cash inflow	£90 000	£120 000
Cost of finance	10%	10%
Time of project	3 yrs	5 yrs

Substituting the information in the NPV formula we have:

Project A

$$NPV = \frac{£90\,000}{(1+0.1)^3} - £40\,000$$

$$NPV = \frac{£90\,000}{(1.1)^3} - £40\,000$$

$$NPV = \frac{£90\,000}{(1.33)} - £40\,000$$

$$NPV = £67\,669 - £40\,000$$

$$NPV = £27\,669$$

Project B

$$NPV = \frac{£120\,000}{(1+0.1)^5} - £50\,000$$

$$NPV = \frac{£120\,000}{(1.1)^5} - £50\,000$$

$$NPV = \frac{£120\,000}{(1.61)} - £50\,000$$

$$NPV = £74\,534 - £50\,000$$

$$NPV = £24\,534$$

It will be seen that by substituting the estimated costs and returns into the NPV formula Project A is the more profitable option. Because both projects are expressed in current money values it allows us to make reliable comparisons between them. Without the application of the formula Project B appears to be the more profitable option.

4.9 Relationships between variables

Relationships between variables occur frequently in business, and such relationships are often represented by the equation $y = \mathrm{b}x + \mathrm{a}$. In this equation x and y represent values which are variable, and b and a are constants which can stand for any given value. When the values of the constants a and b are known then the relationship between x and y can be calculated.

For example, the temperature conversion formula: $F = \frac{9}{5} \times C + 32$ is in the form of $y = \mathrm{b}x + \mathrm{a}$ where $y = F$ and $x = C$ and the two constants ($\mathrm{b} = \frac{9}{5}$; $\mathrm{a} = 32$) are known. So the various relationships between F and C can be calculated. Thus when:

$$x = 0, \quad y = 32$$
$$x = 10, \quad y = 50$$
$$x = 25, \quad y = 77$$

Having obtained three coordinates a graph of a straight line can be drawn. This graph can be used to find all of the related values of centigrade and fahrenheit.

It is important to note that when the values of y are plotted against the corresponding value of x then a straight line graph is obtained. This is true – i.e. a straight line will be obtained – of all graphs of equations of

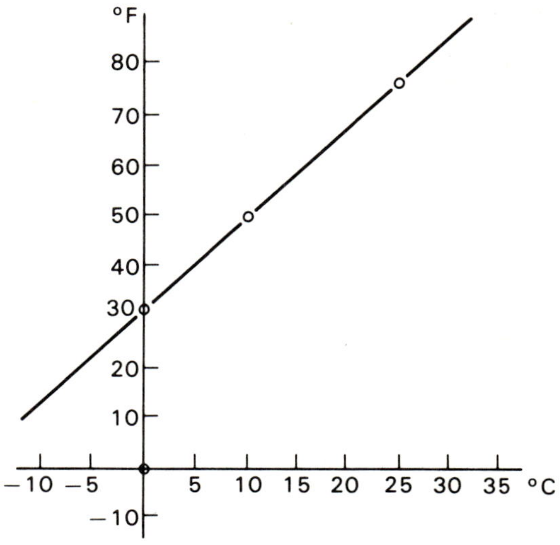

the form $y = bx + a$; and the straight line gives the relationship between the two variables x and y.

4.10 Simultaneous equations

The graphical analysis of equations can be used to solve problems: when two equations are plotted on the same graph, if the two lines intersect, then x and y in both equations will have the same values at the point of intersection. For example, when:

$$y = 2.5x - 1 \quad \text{and} \quad y = 0.5x + 3$$

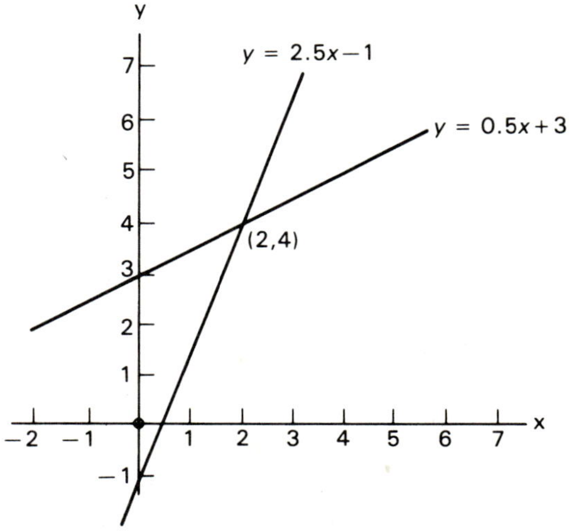

You can see from the graph that the two equations intersect at $x = 2$ and $y = 4$.

These two equations can also be solved using algebra:

$$y = 2.5x - 1 \qquad \text{(i)}$$
$$y = 0.5x + 3 \qquad \text{(ii)}$$

By substituting $y = 0.5x + 3$ into equation (i) we get:

$$0.5x + 3 = 2.5x - 1$$

By rearrangement we get:

$$3 + 1 = 2.5x - 0.5x$$
$$4 = 2x$$
$$x = 2$$

By substituting $x = 2$ into one of the equations we can now find y:

$$y = 2.5x - 1$$
$$y = 2.5\ (2) - 1$$
$$y = 5 - 1$$
$$y = 4$$

Thus $x = 2 y = 4$ is the solution to the two equations.

Exercise 4.10

Solve the following simultaneous equations:

(*a*) $5x - 3y = -5$ and $6x + 2y = 22$
(*b*) $2x + 3y = 43$ and $10x + 4y = 138$
(*c*) $4x + 6y = 11$ and $-3x - y = \frac{1}{2}$
(*d*) $8x - 2y = 5$ and $3x - 5y = -17\frac{1}{4}$
(*e*) $7x - y = 16 + 4y$ and $2x - 6y = 0$

Worked examples

1 The following table gives the rates of exchange in relation to sterling of four different currencies:

£1.00 = 1.850 American dollars
£1.00 = 2.320 Italian lire
£1.00 = 10.80 French francs
£1.00 = 4.250 German marks

(a) Express 40 francs in dollars, and 172 marks in lire.
(b) If a new model Italian car costs 10 million lire and a similar type of German car costs 20 000 marks, using the information given above, determine which car would be cheaper.

Answer

(a) We know that 10.8 francs = 1.85 dollars;
$\therefore$ 1 franc = 1.85/10.8 dollars.

let y = number of dollars
and x = number of francs.

Then $y = \frac{1.85}{10.8}x$.

$\therefore$ when $x = 40$, $y = \frac{1.85}{10.8}(40)$ dollars;

$\therefore$ 40 francs = 6.85 dollars.

Since 4.25 marks = 2320 lire,

then 1 mark $= \frac{2320}{4.25}$ lire.

Let y = number of lire
and x = number of marks.

Then $y = \frac{2320}{4.25}x$.

$\therefore$ when $x = 172$ marks, $y = \frac{2320}{4.25}(172)$ lire;

$\therefore$ 172 marks = 93891.76 lire.

(b) The Italian car costs 10 million lire.
The German car costs 20 000 marks.

We can use the formula $y = \frac{2320}{4.25}x$, which is given above, to convert marks into lire.

In this example $x = 20\,000$ marks

$\therefore y = \frac{2320}{4.25}(20\,000)$ lire = 10 917 647 lire.

The Italian car costs 10 million lire, so it is cheaper than the German car.

2 Given the equation $2 - \sqrt{\frac{5x+4}{4}} = 0$ find the value of x.

Answer

Step 1 Rearrange:

$$2 = \sqrt{\frac{5x+4}{4}}$$

Step 2 Multiply both sides by 4:

$$8 = \sqrt{5x+4}$$

Step 3 Square both sides:

$$64 = 5x + 4$$

Step 4 Subtract 4 from both sides: $60 = 5x$

$$\therefore x = \frac{60}{5} = 12$$

3 The economic-lot size formula is an equation which is used to determine when stocks of raw materials or goods should be re-ordered. The formula is:

$$q = \sqrt{\frac{2eb}{c}}$$

where q = quantity to be ordered;
e = cost of ordering;
b = annual usage;
c = storage cost per unit per annum.

Each year a firm uses 6400 15-inch square steel plates in the production of lawnmowers. The cost of ordering the plate is £12.00, and the cost of storage is £1.50 per plate each year. Substitute the known values into the formula to determine the optimum quantity to be ordered at any one time, then calculate how often an order should be placed. Assume that the firm uses the plates on a continuous basis, and that it operates a 6-day week for 50 weeks each year.

Answer
Substituting the known values into the formula:

$$q = \sqrt{\frac{2 \times 12 \times 6400}{1.5}}$$

$$q = \sqrt{102400} = 320$$

Since the optimum order size is 320 plates and the firm uses an annual total of 6400, then

$$\frac{6400}{320} = 20 \text{ orders have to be placed annually.}$$

The firm operates for 300 days; therefore an order should be placed every

$$\frac{300}{20} = 15 \text{ days.}$$

4 Plot the straight line graph of the two equations:
(a) $y = 5x + 4$
(b) $y = -7x + 2$

Answer

Three points are sufficient to give the co-ordinates of a straight line.

(a) From the equation $y = 5x + 4$:

$$\begin{aligned} \text{when } x &= -2, & y &= -6 \\ x &= 0, & y &= 4 \\ x &= 2, & y &= 14 \end{aligned}$$

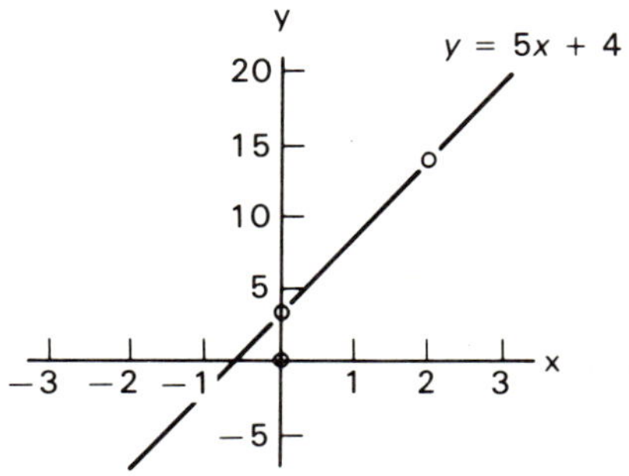

(b) From the equation $y = -7x + 2$:

$$\begin{aligned} \text{when } x &= 0, & y &= 2 \\ x &= 1, & y &= -5 \\ x &= 2, & y &= -12 \end{aligned}$$

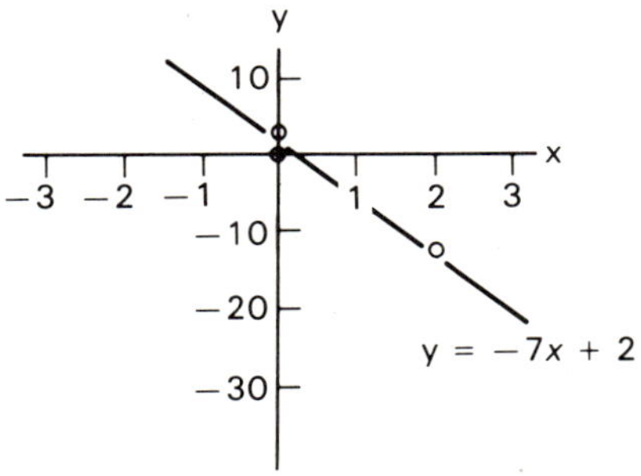

5 The works manager of a small manufacturing company which makes radios in batch production has estimated that the fixed costs incurred in the production of the radios is £4200 and the variable costs are £7.00 per radio.

(a) Assuming that all of the radios produced are sold at £21.00 each, how many radios would have to be manufactured to enable the company to break even?

(b) If production is restricted, so that only 210 radios could be produced and sold, calculate the price that should be charged to enable the company to break even.

Answer

(a) Let x represent the output of radios.
Plot the equations: $y = 21x$ to give revenue from sales
and $y = 7x + 4200$ to give total costs of producing $7x$ radios.

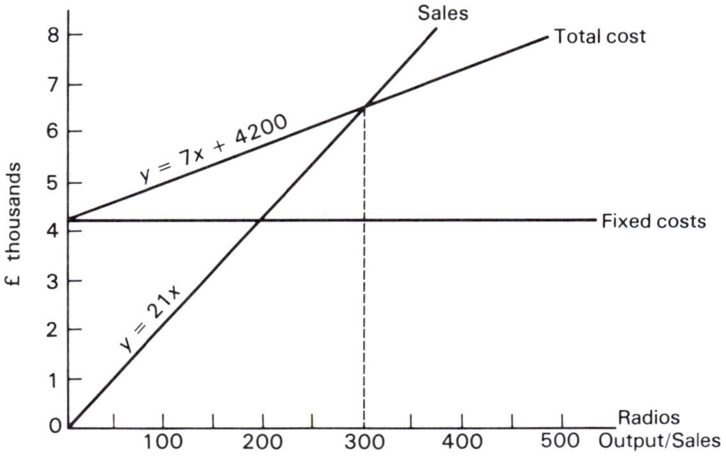

300 radios is the break-even point.

(b) Since $y = 7x + 4200$
when $x = 210$,
then $y = 1470 + 4200 = 5670$
$\therefore$ the total costs incurred in the production of 210 radios = £5670;
$\therefore$ the price of one radio to be charged to cover total cost $= £\frac{5670}{210}$

= £27.00.

The price to be charged to break even when 210 are produced and sold is £27.00.

6 A supplier of animal feeds mixes wheat, maize gluten, and tapioca in varying proportions:

Mix A contains 60% wheat and the remainder is made up of equal proportions of maize gluten and tapioca. The cost of mix A is £120 per ton.

In mix B, if the supplier uses 70% wheat and the remainder contains twice as much tapioca as maize gluten, then the mix costs £107 per ton.

Assuming that maize gluten costs twice as much as tapioca find the cost per ton of each of the constituents of the mixes.

Answer
Let the cost of wheat be £x per ton, the cost of tapioca be £y per ton, and the cost of maize gluton be £z per ton.

Mix A contains 60% wheat and the remaining 40% is made up of equal parts of maize gluten and tapioca – i.e. 20% each – and the cost per ton is £120. This gives the equation:

$$0.6x + 0.2y + 0.2z = 120 \quad \text{(i)}$$

Mix B contains 70% wheat and the remaining 30% contains twice as much tapioca as maize gluten – i.e. 20% tapioca and 10% maize gluten – and the cost of the feed is £107 per ton. This gives the equation:

$$0.7x + 0.2y + 0.1z = 107 \quad \text{(ii)}$$

Finally we know that maize gluten costs twice as much as tapioca; therefore

$$z = 2y$$

By substituting $z = 2y$ into the two equations, we get:

$$0.6x + 0.6y = 120 \quad \text{(iii)}$$

$$0.7x + 0.4y = 107 \quad \text{(iv)}$$

By expressing x in terms of y in equation (iii) we get

$$0.6x = 120 - 0.6y$$

$$\therefore x = 200 - y.$$

If we then substitute this value of x into equation (iv):

$$\begin{aligned} 0.7(200 - y) + 0.4y &= 107 \\ 140 - 0.7y + 0.4y &= 107 \\ 3y &= 330 \\ y &= 110 \\ \text{since } z &= 2y \\ \text{then } z &= 220 \end{aligned}$$

Substitute $y = 110$ and $z = 220$ into equation (i).

$$\begin{aligned} 0.6x + 0.2(110) + 0.2(220) &= 120 \\ 0.6x = 120 - 22 - 44 &= 54 \\ \therefore x = \frac{54}{0.6} &= 90 \end{aligned}$$

The price of wheat is £90 per ton, tapioca £110 per ton, and maize gluten £220 per ton.

Additional exercises

1 (a) In the equation $q = p + bx$
(i) What is the value of p if $q = 100$, $b = 4$ and $x = 12$?
(ii) What is the value of x if $q = 140$, $b = 5$ and $p = 90$?

(b) In the equation $m = \sqrt{\dfrac{y(x-y)}{n^2}}$
(i) What is the value of m if $x = 2.5$, $y = 0.5$ and $n = 2$?
(ii) What is the value of n if $x = 13$, $y = 4$ and $m = 3$?

2 Change the equation $x = \sqrt{\dfrac{m-9}{2y}}$ so that y is the subject of the equation.

3 Draw the graph of the following equations:
(a) $y = 2.5x + 3$
(b) $x = 4.6 - 3.2y$
(c) $7.2 = 10y - 4x$

4 As an office manager you are about to transfer your department into a new office. The architect has provided the following incomplete details of the dimensions of the office:

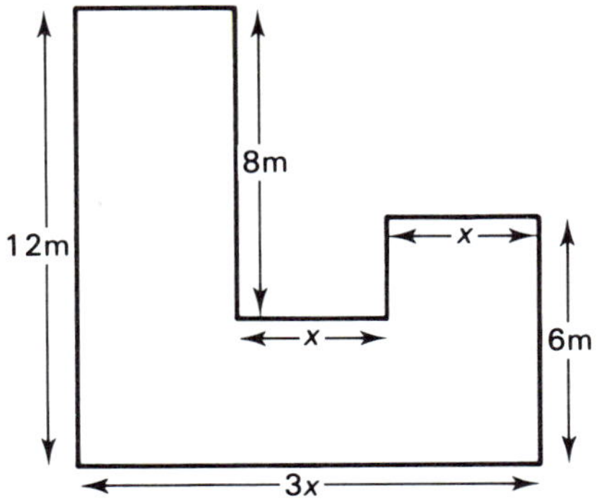

(a) If the total area of the new office is 88 square metres find the value of x.
(b) Calculate the area of the office if $x = 7$ metres.

5 Solve the following simultaneous equations:
(a) $3x + 4y = 39$ and $5x - 2y = 13$
(b) $3y - 0.5x = 6$ and $6y - 5x = 0$
(c) $2a + 3b = 15$ and $3a = 7b + 4$

6 The price of a product influences the demand for that product, and economists have derived a formula which measures the degree of influence of price on demand. It is known as the *price elasticity of demand* equation:

$$e = \frac{q_2 - q_1}{q_1} \cdot \frac{p_2 - p_1}{p_1}$$

where e = price elasticity of demand
q_1 = % quantity demanded in period 1
q_2 = % quantity demanded in period 2
p_1 = % price in period 1
p_2 = % price in period 2

The following table shows how a decrease in the price of eggs influenced the demand for eggs during the first two quarters of a year:

	Jan/March	*April/June*
Price of eggs (%)	100	80
Quantity of eggs demanded %	100	120

(a) Use the formula given above to calculate the price elasticity of demand for eggs.
(b) Assuming that the price/demand relationship remains constant, calculate what the proportionate fall in demand would be if the price of eggs increased by 15% over the same period.

7 A road haulage firm wants to replace its fleet of 6 vehicles and is considering two proposals:
Proposal X Purchase of 6 vehicles at £12 000 each. The estimated repair and maintenance costs are £118 per quarter for each vehicle; and the supplier of the new vehicles would allow £2000 in part exchange for each of the old ones.
Proposal Y Leasing of 6 vehicles at £708 each per quarter. This price would include all repair and maintenance costs; and the directors of the haulage company estimate that each of the existing fleet of vehicles could be sold for £1800 cash.

Using the information given above calculate by graphical means how long it would be before the cost of leasing exceeded the cost of purchasing the vehicle.

8 A retailer in electrical appliances stocks two brands of electric toaster. His accountant has calculated from rough records that when 6 brand A toasters and 5 brand B toasters were sold the overall profit was £65.00. He also knows when the retailer sold 8 brand A and six brand B toasters that the total profit was £82.00.

From this information calculate the profit on each individual brand.

5 Collection of data and tabulation

5.1 Introduction

Data or statistics are available on almost every aspect of life – population, economics, sport, etc. Some statistics, such as those in the *Guinness Book of Records*, are collected mainly because they enable us to make interesting and entertaining comparisons. But organisations collect data in such areas as sales, production, and personnel so that the activities of the organisation can be measured and controlled.

Quite a lot of the statistics in business are of a financial nature dealing primarily with balance sheets and profit and loss accounts. However this section deals mainly with non-financial data, and financial information is explained in chapters 10–14.

5.2 Primary data

Initially all information has to be collected in its raw state. The collection or compilation of primary data can range from very exacting methods using questionnaires, such as those used in the government's demographic surveys, to rough guesses such as an estimate of the numbers attending a political rally in central London. Naturally, the reliability of any analysis or usage of the data depends on the accuracy of the collection.

The most obvious type of primary data that is collected in business is the information which organisations automatically record in order to administer the business efficiently, such as details of employees, sales and production figures, and stock records. But organisations sometimes collect other forms of primary data. For example many firms collect marketing information through market research organisations, and some have their own research departments which collect data for scientific purposes.

The important point to remember is that all organisations, no matter how small, will produce primary data of some kind.

5.3 Secondary data

All data, when first collected, is primary data; and, as we have seen in section 5.2, primary data is collected for a specific purpose. Primary data can, of course, be used for additional purposes. For example absentee records, which a firm might keep to ensure that employees are correctly paid, could be analysed by university research workers who are examining the causes of absenteeism. When statistics are used in this secondary fashion they are described as secondary data. Secondary data, therefore, is data which was originally collected for some other purpose.

A main source of secondary data is the government. Each government department has a statistics division which produces specialised statistics such as 'transport statistics' or 'energy statistics' for administrative purposes. Such statistics are published, and the main summary of government published statistics is the *Annual Abstract of Statistics for the United Kingdom*, which is produced by the Central Statistical Office in collaboration with the government departments.

The following list of the chapter headings from the *Annual Abstract* illustrates how extensive the government's statistical service, and therefore this form of secondary data, is:

Area and climate
Population and vital statistics
Social conditions
Education
Labour
Defence
Production
Distributive trades and services
External trade
Balance of payments
National income and expenditure
Personal income, expenditure and wealth
Home finance
Banking, insurance, etc.
Prices

5.4 Raw data

Raw data is statistical information that has not been processed and presented in the form of a table or diagram. Thus primary data immediately after its collection is raw data.

In almost all statistical surveys the raw data which is collected is too numerous to be easily analysed and understood. Therefore the first task, after the collection stage, is to classify and tabulate the information.

The following example of raw data is a record of height, to the nearest centimetre, of 60 policemen employed at a central police station:

184	192	172	168	173	185	187	193	186	182
183	181	174	183	187	190	184	175	184	189
186	185	181	184	172	175	179	189	185	186
184	174	182	179	188	181	189	188	177	179
174	175	184	186	179	175	177	185	182	181
178	185	186	184	177	179	179	182	178	181

It is clear that it is difficult to make much sense of data in this raw form. However, a simple classification of the policemen's heights enables us to present the information so that it is easier to understand.

5.5 Classification of raw data

The first task in classification is to find out how often each variable occurs (i.e. the *frequency* with which each variable occurs). For example, using the raw data from section 5.4 we get the following frequency distribution:

Variable *height* (*cm*)	*Frequency* *men* (*no.*)	*Variable* *height* (*cm*)	*Frequency* *men* (*no.*)
168 /	1	181 ~~////~~	5
169	0	182 ////	4
170	0	183 //	2
171	0	184 ~~////~~ //	7
172 //	2	185 ~~////~~	5
173 /	1	186 ~~////~~	5
174 ///	3	187 //	2
175 ////	4	188 //	2
176	0	189 ///	3
177 ///	3	190 /	1
178 //	2	191	0
179 ~~////~~ /	6	192 /	1
180	0	193 /	1

Although this frequency table shows how often each variable occurs, the table is still too long to be easily understood. However, the information can be condensed by grouping the variables into classes, which will help us to make the data even more manageable and assist us in the presentation of the information.

For example, if we group the above data into five classes it will give us the following grouped frequency distribution:

height (*cm*)	*men* (*no.*)
less than 175	7
175–179	15
180–184	18
185–189	17
more than 189	3
Total	60

When the information is presented in this form it is relatively easy to draw conclusions about the data. For example, we can see that 18/60 (30 %) of the policemen are in the narrow range 180–184 cm; and that only 3/60 (5 %) exceed 189 cm.

In this example the class width or class interval remains constant at 5 cm. The height of the men was measured to the nearest cm so a height of 179.8 cm would have been recorded as 180 cm. Thus the true class limits of the class 180–184 are actually 179.5–184.5. This rounding process applies to each of the classes and gives us a class width of 5 cm in each case.

The following rules will help you to classify raw data:

(1) Ensure that all the data is included in the classes.

(2) The classes should be large enough to eliminate irrelevant detail, but not so large that too much information is lost. For example, if, in the classification given above, we had used three classes rather than five we would have:

height (*cm*)	*men* (*no.*)
less than 175	7
175–184	33
more than 184	20

In this case the classes are too large, and it is more difficult to see how the heights of the 60 policemen are distributed throughout the range of the data.

(3) Each variable should be classified only once. Class limits should not overlap; this will ensure that there is no confusion when classifying each unit. So an ambiguous classification, such as the following, should be avoided: less than 175; 175–180; 180–185; 185–190; more than 190.

5.6 Tabulation

One of the most common methods of presenting business information is in the form of a table; and it is important to be able to read and evaluate information which is in tabular form. A table is, in effect, an extended method of classification; and therefore the rules of classification apply to tabulation.

The frequency distribution table, which is given in section 5.5, is an example of a simple table. The information about the police could have been far more complex – for example, the variables could have been divided into additional categories such as age, sex, or status – and this would have created a more complicated form of tabulation. Since tables can be complex it is useful, when constructing and interpreting tables, to bear in mind some basic points.

All tables consist of rows and columns of data plus additional relevant information. The basic rules of tabulation are:

(1) The table should have an explanatory title.
(2) Each row and column should have a heading which explains how the data is classified.
(3) The units of measurement should be clearly shown.
(4) Totals and sub-totals should be shown when they are appropriate.
(5) Footnotes should be used to give further explanation or definition. For example, it might be necessary to define some data categories such as 'net income'.
(6) Any sources should be acknowledged.

The following diagram illustrates the general layout of a table:

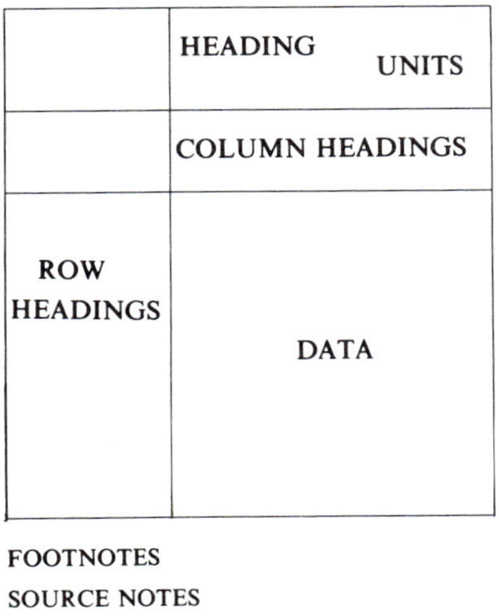

5.7 Interpreting tables

Table 5.1* is included because it is a good example of how a table should be constructed.

* From *Social Trends*, 1983 (HMSO).

Table 5.1 Population changes and projections: *United Kingdom*
(millions and thousands)

	Population at start of period (millions)	*Average annual change (thousands)*				
		Live births	*Deaths*	*Net natural change*	*Net civilian migration and other adjustments*	*Overall annual change*
Census enumerated						
1901–11	38.2	1091	624	467	−82	385
1911–21	42.1	975	689	286	−92	194
1921–31	44.0	824	555	268	−67	201
1931–51	46.0	785	598	188	+25	213
Mid-year estimates						
1951–61	50.3	839	593	246	+ 6	252
1961–66	52.8	988	633	355	−15	339
1966–71	54.5	937	644	293	−71	222
1971–72	55.6	862	661	202	−30	171
1972–73	55.8	808	672	136	− 4	132
1973–74	55.9	752	664	88	−78	10
1974–75	55.9	721	671	50	−71	−22
1975–76	55.9	689	681	7	−22	−15
1976–77	55.9	655	660	−5	−28	−33
1977–78	55.9	664	665	—	−17	−17
1978–79	55.8	720	672	48	− 2	46
1979–80	55.9	743	658	86	−22	64
1980–81	55.9	738[2]	659[2]	79[2]	—	—
Projections[1]						
1981–86	56.0	813	705	108	−29	79
1986–91	56.4	901	716	185	−30	155
1991–96	57.2	896	717	179	−30	149
1996–2001	57.9	827	710	117	−30	87

[1] Projections based on mid-1979 estimate of total population.
[2] Provisional.
Sources: Office of Population Censuses and Surveys; Government Actuary's Department; General Register Office (Scotland); General Register Office (Northern Ireland).

The basic rules for the construction of tables – given in section 5.6–also provide a framework for interpreting tabular information. For example, in Table 5.1 the data is classified in rows into three distinctive headings which show the actual census 1901–51, the mid-year estimates 1951–81, and projections 1981–2001. There are two main column types: the total population in millions, and then a division of the average annual change into several additional columns which are expressed in thousands. Apart from the second to last and last columns there are no totals or sub-totals because they are not appropriate. The footnotes provide further explanation of the data, and the sources of the raw data are acknowledged.

Having examined the construction of the table we are in a position to interpret the data; and there are many conclusions we could draw from this one table. For instance we can see how the decline in live births during the 1970s affected the relative growth in the total population, and how net migration has almost always been negative.

Worked example

The following details are taken from the personnel records of MSM Ltd during one trading year beginning 1 January.

At the beginning of the period the firm employed 6562 people, of which 4427 were men, 1587 were women and the remainder were trainees of both sexes. During the period 215 men and 324 women resigned, 198 men and 302 women were engaged, and the number of trainees increased by 37. The average weekly wage paid to the men was £126.26, to the women £82.69, and to the trainees £48.92. The absentee records for the period show that the number of days lost through illness were 10 206 for men, 4523 for women and 1268 for the trainees. In addition to these days lost through illness the records show the following number of days lost for other reasons: men 1255, women 547 and trainees 102.

You are required to construct a table which includes all of the information and shows totals and sub-totals. The table should show the number employed at the end of the period, and the weekly wage bill, in each category, at the beginning and the end of the period.

Answer

MSM LTD PERSONNEL RECORDS, 1 January–31 December 19xx

	Men	*Women*	*Trainees*	*Totals*
Employment (actual)				
Total 1 Jan	4 427	1 587	548	6 562
Less resignations	(−215)	(−324)		
Add engagements	(+198)	(+302)		
Net changes	−17	−22	+37	
Total 31 Dec	4 410	1 565	585	6 560
Wages (£)				
Total 1 Jan	558 953	131 229	26 808	716 990
Total 31 Dec	556 807	129 410	28 618	714 835
Absenteeism (no of days lost)				
Illness	10 206	4 523	1 268	15 997
Other reasons	1 255	547	102	1 904
Total	11 461	5 070	1 370	17 901

Exercises

1 The following information was collected as part of a social survey into education and unemployment in a large urban area:

(a) The total population of the area was 456 000.
(b) 58% of the population was female.
(c) 68 000 females and 41 000 males were aged 16 and under.
(d) 88 000 females were aged 60 years and over, and 49 000 males were aged 65 and over.

(e) 10 % of the female population and 9 % of the male population were aged between 16 and 21 years. 20 % of this age group were in full-time further and higher education; 25 % were unemployed.
(f) 8 % of females aged between 21 and 60 years, and 15 % of males aged between 21 and 65 years were registered as unemployed.

Tabulate this data and calculate any additional statistics which will enable you to present the information in a comprehensive form.

2 A building society is conducting a survey into the proportional distribution of its loans during a 5-year period. The society is particularly interested in the different amounts which have been borrowed in relation to age of the property. It decides to analyse the information in five classifications of amount loaned: up to £5000; £5000–£10 000; £10 000–£15 000; £15 000–£25 000; and more than £25 000. The categories of age of property which it has decided upon are less than 5 years; 5–10 years; 10–25 years; 25–50 years; and more than 50 years.
(a) Prepare a table in which the data could be presented cross-classification by year, size of loan, and age of the property.
(b) Insert the following data into the appropriate part of the table:
(i) In the first year 35 % of loans less than £5000 were on properties which were less than 5 years old.
(ii) In the third year 82 % of the loans of over £25 000 were on properties aged more than 50 years.
(iii) In the fifth year 17 % of the loans of £10 000–£15 000 were on properties built 20–25 years ago.

3 You are required to write a newspaper article which is entitled 'Population and population density: international comparisons'. The basis for your article should be the information which is included in Table 5.2* on p. 51.

Your article should be between 800 and 1000 words; and, in addition, you can reproduce the whole or parts of the table. You should assume that the readers of the newspaper know very little about international population figures, and that they are not familiar with detailed tabular information. The prime objective is to select and explain the most interesting comparisons which can be drawn from the data.

4 A firm which offers security services decides to impose a minimum height requirement of 175 cm for all new recruits. There are 250 applicants for new positions and their heights have been measured to the nearest cm. The smallest is 164 cms and the tallest is 189 cm.
(a) The personnel manager assumes that the heights are evenly distributed and decides, therefore, that 44 % of the applicants should be rejected. Comment on this decision.

* From *Social Trends*, 1983 (HMSO).

Table 5.2 Population and population density: international comparison

	Estimates of mid-year population (millions)						Percentage change	Population density (number per square km)
	1961	*1966*	*1971*	*1976*	*1980*	*1981*	*1971–81*	*1981*
United Kingdom	52.8	54.7	55.6	55.9	55.9	55.9	0.5	229
Belgium	9.2	9.5	9.7	9.8	9.9	9.9	2.1	319
Denmark	4.6	4.8	5.0	5.1	5.1	5.1	2.0	119
France	46.2	49.4	51.2	52.9	53.7	54.0	5.5	99
Germany (FRG)[1]	56.2	59.7	61.3	61.5	61.6	61.7	0.7	248
Greece	8.4	8.6	8.8	9.2	9.6	9.7	10.2	73
Irish Republic	2.8	2.9	3.0	3.2	3.4	3.4	13.3	49
Italy	49.9	52.0	54.0	56.2	57.1	57.2	5.9	190
Luxembourg	0.3	0.3	0.3	0.4	0.4	0.4	33.3	133
Netherlands	11.6	12.4	13.2	13.8	14.1	14.2	7.6	346
European Community[2]	242.0	254.3	262.1	268.0	270.8	271.5	3.6	163
Portugal	8.9	9.3	9.0	9.7	9.9	9.9	10.0	108
Spain	30.6	31.9	34.1	36.0	37.4	37.6	10.3	74
Turkey	28.2	31.9	36.2	41.1	44.9	46.4	28.2	59
Sweden	7.5	7.8	8.1	8.2	8.3	8.3	2.5	18
Australia	10.5	11.5	12.9	13.9	14.6	14.9	15.5	2
Canada	18.3	20.0	21.6	23.0	24.0	24.2	12.0	2
New Zealand	2.4	2.7	2.8	3.1	3.1	3.1	10.7	12
USA	183.8	196.9	206.2	215.1	227.7	229.8	11.4	25
Brazil	71.8	83.2	95.2	109.2	118.6	121.6	27.7	14
China	671.0	722.8	840.0	908.3	994.9	1,007.8	20.0	105
India	439.0	498.7	551.3	613.3	663.6	683.8	24.0	208
Japan[3]	94.0	98.9	105.7	112.8	116.8	117.6	11.3	316
USSR	218.0	233.1	245.1	256.7	265.5	267.7	9.2	12

[1] Includes West Berlin.
[2] Includes United Kingdom, Irish Republic, Denmark, and Greece
[3] Includes Okinawa.
Sources: United Nations Demographic Year Book 1979; UN Monthly Bulletin of Statistics.

(b) Give the class limits of a distribution with 6 classes into which this range of heights could be grouped.

5 A survey of the weekly earnings of 12 600 members of a trade union, who describe their posts as 'clerical officers', gives the following results:

Weekly gross earnings (£)	*Number of members*
under 90	86
90–94	310
95–99	1240
100–104	2208
105–109	2846
110–114	3000
115–119	1824
120–124	610
125–129	360
130 or more	116

You are required to determine the number of members who earn:
(a) at least £105;
(b) more than £120;
(c) less than £100;
(d) at most £105;
(e) £119 or less.

6 Diagrammatic presentation of data

6.1 Introduction

We have noted already that it is often very difficult to understand statistical information when it is presented in its raw form. Diagrams, like tabulation (chapter 5) and graphs (chapter 7), provide us with methods of presenting business information. The main reason for using diagrams is that they enable us to bring out the main features of the data in a simple and interesting way.

The main problem in representing data in this way is that some of the detail in the information is inevitably lost. Diagrams provide approximations from which general conclusions can be drawn.

The illustrations used in this chapter, which are taken from government publications, have been included because they show the range of different forms which can be used.

6.2 Simple bar chart

A bar chart is one of the best methods of presenting information; it is relatively easy to construct and at the same time is easy to understand. The length of bar is proportional to the quantity it represents. However, it is important that each bar should have the same width so that only the length of bar is compared.

Worked example

Using the information given in Table 6.1* draw a simple bar chart which shows the 'Identifiable public expenditure, 1980/81' for each of the following services:

(a) Health and personal social services;
(b) Education and science, arts and libraries;
(c) Housing;
(d) Other environmental services;
(e) Law, order and protective services.

* From *Regional Trends*, 1982 (HMSO).

Table 6.1 Identifiable public expenditure per head

(£ per head)[1]

	1979/80				1980/81[2]			
	England	*Wales*	*Scotland*	*N. Ireland*	*England*	*Wales*	*Scotland*	*N. Ireland*
Agriculture, fisheries, food and forestry	12	23	31	69	13	28	38	75
Industry, energy, trade and employment	35	79	75	199	52	127	101	237
Government lending to nationalised industries	23	96	42	−4	43	306	90	—
Roads and transport	49	80	73	74	56	97	88	79
Housing	105	81	151	139	107	81	155	158
Other environmental services	62	81	91	67	71	90	104	79
Law, order and protective services	51	42	54	164	63	52	67	204
Education and science; arts and libraries	195	202	235	253	233	247	293	297
Health and personal social services	192	195	239	248	246	252	301	314
Social security	347	365	362	385	423	437	405	463
Other public services	17	27	34	18	20	31	42	23
Common services	10	8	8	13	11	9	11	18
Total	1098	1279	1393	1625	1339	1759	1696	1946

[1] Figures are independently rounded and may not sum to totals.
[2] Provisional.
Source: H.M. Treasury.

*Answer**

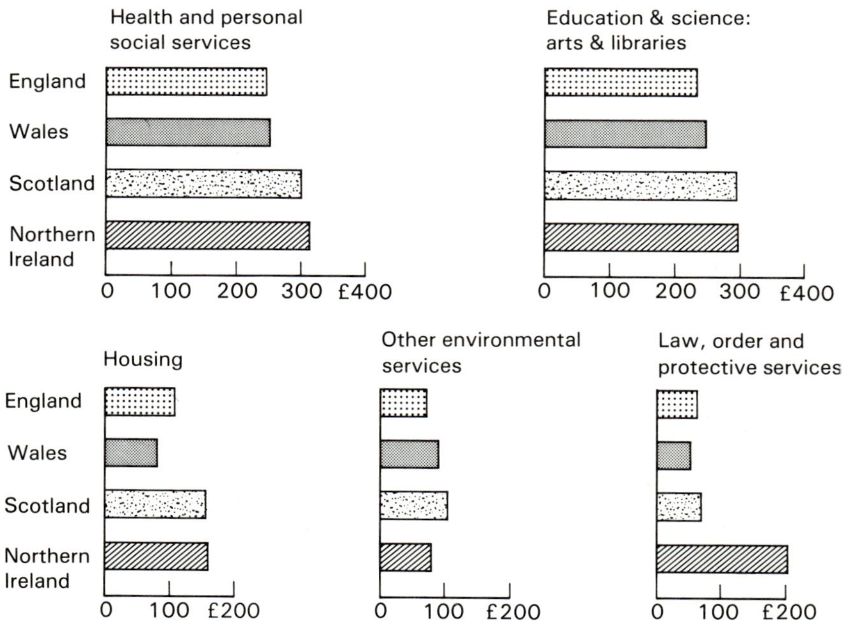

Figure 6.1 Identifiable public expenditure, 1980/81 (£ per head)

* From *Regional Trends*, 1982 (HMSO).

6.3 Gain and loss bar chart

An advantage of a bar chart is that it can represent negative, as well as positive, numbers. We can show gains and losses on the same chart as Figure 6.2* illustrates.

Figure 6.2 Annual changes in real household disposable income[1] per head

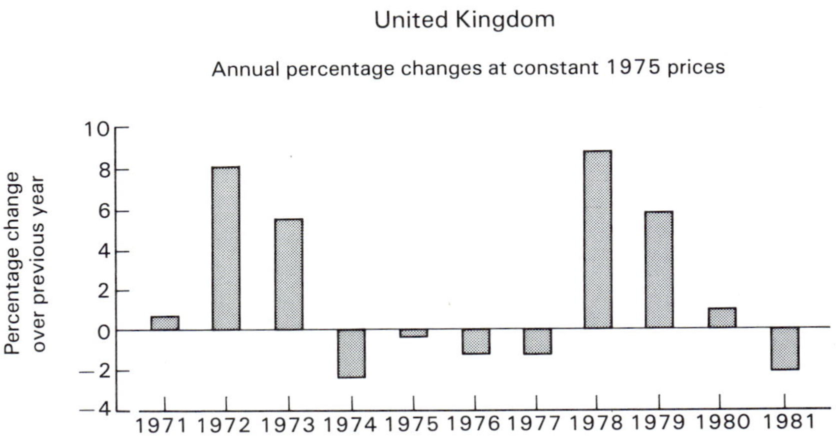

[1]Year by year percentage changes in household income, after allowing for tax and inflation

Source: Central Statistical Office

Gain and loss bar charts should be kept simple: if too much information is included within the one bar (see Section 6.5) then it could be difficult to show the extent of gains and losses.

6.4 Multiple bar chart

A multiple bar chart is a collection of simple bar charts in the same diagram. Multiple bar charts are appropriate when the data is within several classes, and shading or colour is then used to denote each class. Figure 6.3** has five classes of income and shows male and female separately. Comparisons would be much more difficult if the two charts were combined, or if the income group had been divided into smaller – and therefore more – classes.

* From *Social Trends*, 1982 (HMSO).
** From *Social Trends*, 1983 (HMSO).

Figure 6.3 Educational establishment last attended full-time: by sex and usual gross weekly earnings,[1] 1981

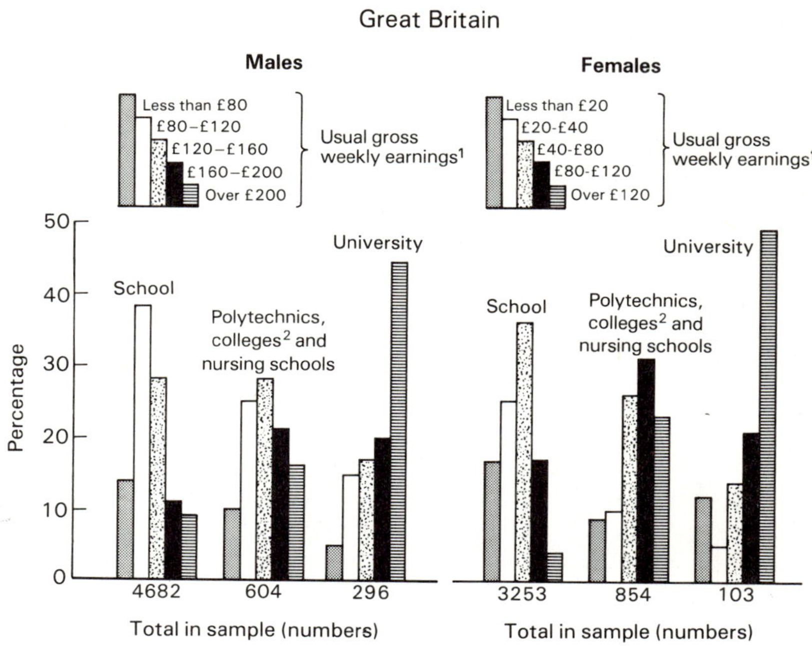

[1]Earnings of people aged 20-64 currently in full-time or part-time employment but not in full-time or part-time education

[2]Colleges of further education (including colleges of education in Scotland, Northern Ireland and outside the United Kingdom, as well as former colleges of education in England and Wales) and other colleges

Source: General Household Survey. 1981

6.5 Component bar chart

A component bar chart shows how a total is split into its various parts, and it enables us to compare totals. It is difficult to compare the components within a total; nevertheless such a chart does allow us to make an estimate of changes in the component structure of each bar.

Figure 6.4* illustrates these two features. It is easy to see the total change in trade union membership for each year; but it is more difficult to assess the changes within the totals. Nevertheless on closer examination we are able to see such changes as the decline in the smaller unions and the growth of very large unions.

* From *Social Trends*, 1983 (HMSO).

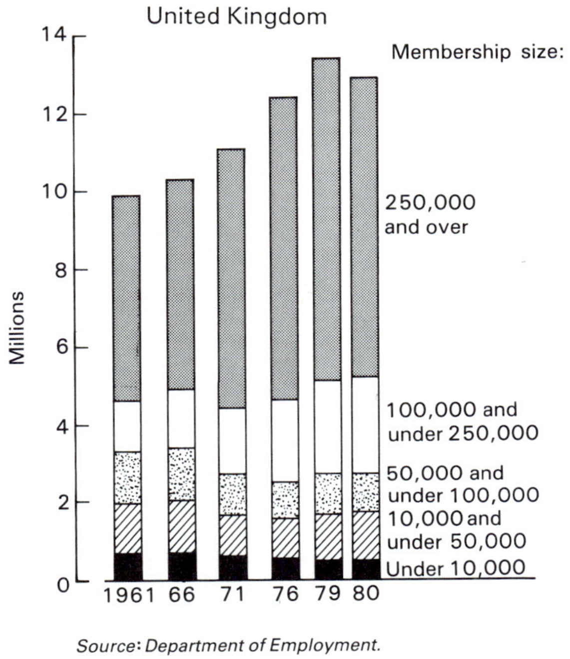

Figure 6.4 Trade union membership by size of union

6.6 Percentage component bar chart

The difficulty in comparing the components between bars is overcome, to some extent, by the percentage component bar chart which shows the percentage change within each bar. The length of each bar represents 100 %; and the components are shown as proportions of the total. The actual total figures are normally written in against the respective bar. Figure 6.5* provides an example.

6.7 Pie chart

A pie chart represents information by showing a circle divided into sections. It is often used in the same way as a percentage component bar chart in that it shows how a total is divided into its various proportions. Figure 6.6 is an example of a pie chart.**

A pie chart is an interesting method of representing data, but it has limitations:

* From *Social Trends*, 1983 (HMSO).

* From *Regional Trends*, 1982 (HMSO).

Figure 6.5 Unemployment[1]: by sex and occupation

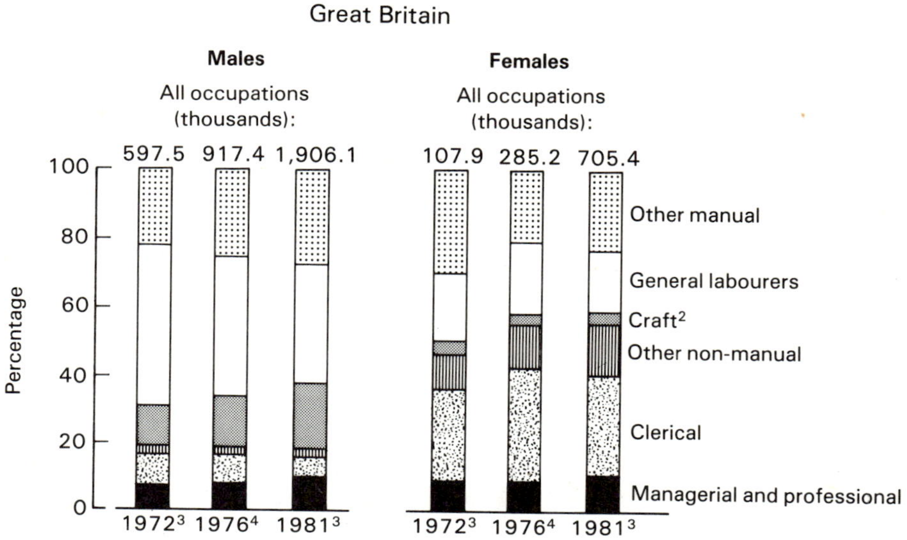

[1]Excluding school leavers and people without an occupation
[2]Craft and similar occupations (including foremen) in processing, production, repairing etc.
[3]At December
[4]At September

Source: Department of Employment.

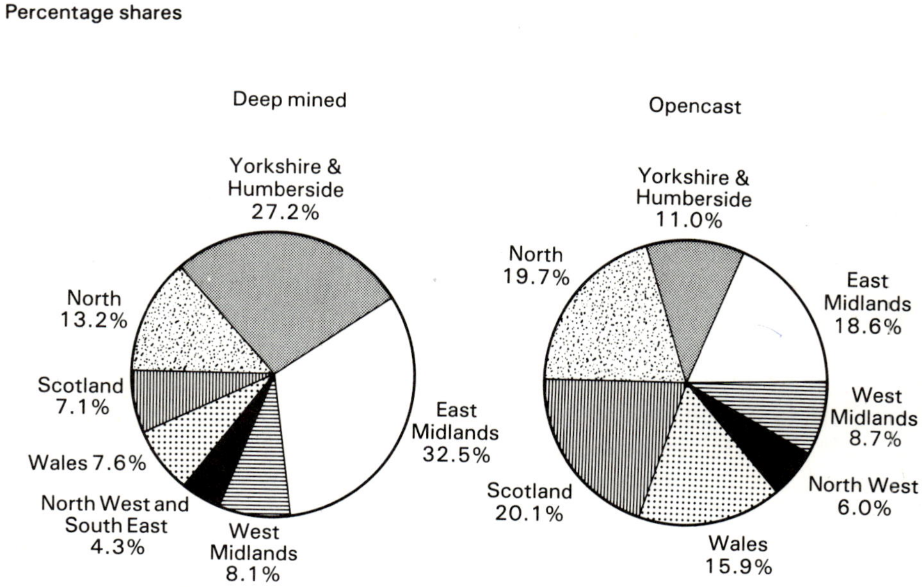

Figure 6.6 Production of coal, 1980/81 (55)

(a) Since a circle is divided into degrees it can be cumbersome to calculate the size of each segment: the proportion has to be calculated and then converted into degrees by multiplying by 360 (see worked example).
(b) Similarly it can be difficult to mark each segment accurately.
(c) Some people feel that it is difficult to assess the relative size of each segment.
(d) Circles that have different total values pose additional problems: not only are they relatively difficult to construct but they are not easily compared. You can test the extent of this difficulty by examining the two circles given below and deciding whether A is twice as big or three times as big as B.

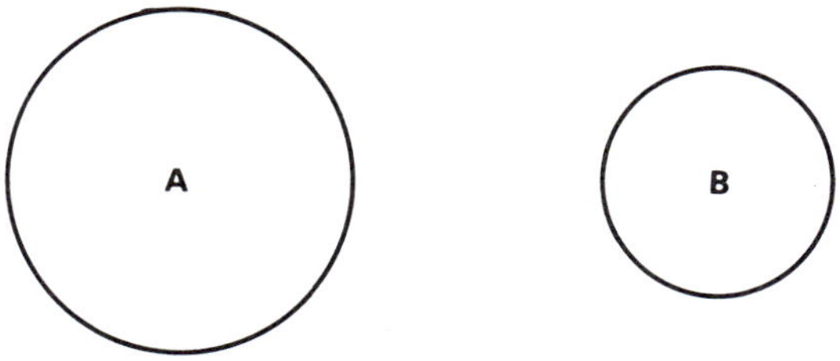

Because of these disadvantages it is generally better to use a percentage component bar chart than a pie chart.

6.8 Pictograms and cartograms

Sometimes pictures or drawings are used to represent information. For instance a map or cartogram is used when geographical location is an important aspect of the data. Figure 6.7 is one such example.

Pictures or drawings are used when it is felt necessary to make the chart easy to understand. But, like pie charts, pictograms and cartograms are not easy to construct; and they can be difficult to interpret accurately.

6.9 Conclusions

The purpose of representing information in the form of charts or diagrams is to convey the main details of any data. It is fair to assume that most people can judge linear comparisons better than other diagrammatic comparisons. Therefore, generally it is more advisable to use bar charts – simple, multiple, component – than other methods of representation.

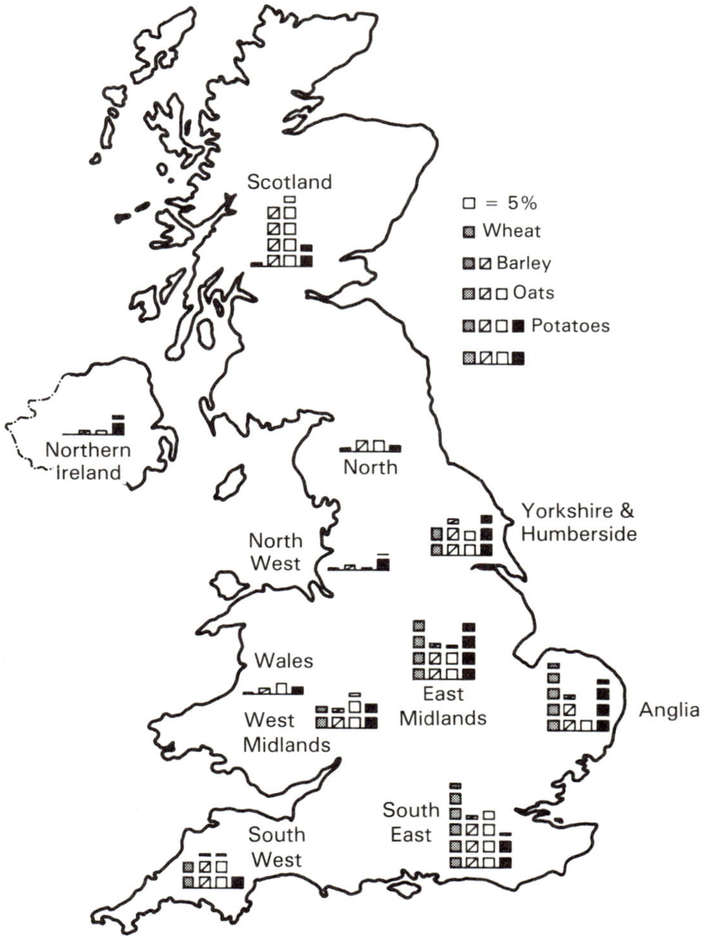

Figure 6.7 Production of selected crops, 1980 harvest, as percentage of UK production

Worked example

Using the information provided in Table 6.2* construct:

(a) component bar charts; and
(b) pie charts that show the total imports and exports from the regions of England.

* From *Regional Trends*, 1982 (HMSO).

Table 6.2 Foreign trade: imports and exports, 1980

(a) *Imports* (thousand tonnes)

	Total	*Food stuffs*	*Basic mat-erials*	*Petro-leum*	*Manu-fac-tured goods*	*Coal*
Great Britain Seaports	131 897	16 270	25 061	57 976	24 989	7 601
North	10 181	376	4 271	2 318	1 890	1 326
Yorkshire and Humberside	16 872	1 170	5 330	6 062	4 068	243
East Midlands	666	48	75	—	535	7
East Anglia	5 287	1 241	648	105	3 217	75
South East	49 513	7 115	5 308	24 342	10 214	2 533
South West	3 986	1 384	1 314	165	1 026	96
North West	10 566	3 095	2 158	2 472	1 656	1 186
England	97 070	14 429	19 104	35 465	22 606	5 466
Wales	24 590	616	2 816	18 633	999	1 526
Scotland	10 237	1 225	3 140	3 878	1 385	608

(b) *Exports* (thousand tonnes)

	Total	*Food-stuffs*	*Basic mat-erials*	*Petro-leum*	*Manu-fac-tured goods*	*Coal*
Great Britain Seaports	117 448	6 973	9 236	74 896	21 070	5 272
North	25 415	268	1 126	20 392	2 431	1 198
Yorkshire and Humberside	8 536	861	456	1 953	2 693	2 573
East Midlands	297	185	23	1	66	24
East Anglia	4 176	1 324	503	76	2 270	4
South East	15 774	2 045	1 403	4 283	8 037	7
South West	4 482	748	3 251	6	472	5
North West	6 035	467	944	1 133	3 341	150
England	64 715	5 898	7 706	27 843	19 308	3 960
Wales	10 656	236	907	7 173	1 048	1 292
Scotland	42 078	839	624	39 880	713	21

Source: Department of Transport.

Answer

(a)

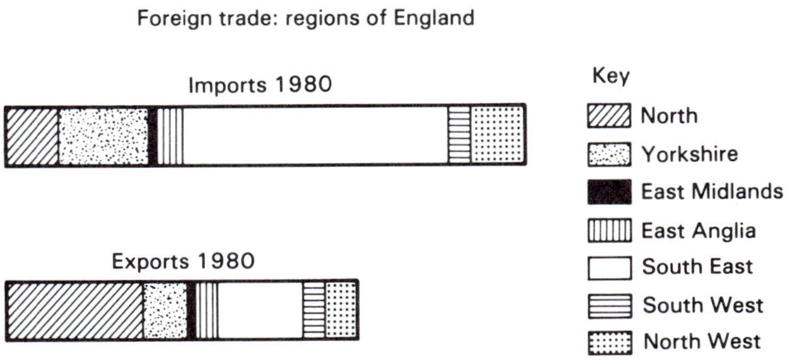

Figure 6.8 Foreign trade: regions of England (component bar chart)

(b) Pie chart segment calculations (degrees):

	Imports	*Exports*
North	$\frac{10.1}{97.1} \times 360 = 37$	$\frac{25.4}{64.7} \times 360 = 141$
Yorkshire	$\frac{16.9}{97.1} \times 360 = 63$	$\frac{8.5}{64.7} \times 360 = 47$
East Midlands	$\frac{0.7}{97.1} \times 360 = 3$	$\frac{0.3}{64.7} \times 360 = 2$
East Anglia	$\frac{5.3}{97.1} \times 360 = 20$	$\frac{4.1}{64.7} \times 360 = 23$
South East	$\frac{49.5}{97.1} \times 360 = 183$	$\frac{15.8}{64.7} \times 360 = 88$
South West	$\frac{4.0}{97.1} \times 360 = 15$	$\frac{4.5}{64.7} \times 360 = 25$
North West	$\frac{10.6}{97.1} \times 360 = 39$	$\frac{6.1}{64.7} \times 360 = 34$

Figure 6.9 Foreign trade: regions of England (pie chart)

Exercises

1 Using the information in Table 6.3 construct multiple bar charts which show the attendance at football matches in the four divisions and Scotland for the three seasons 1961/62, 1971/72, and 1981/82.

Table 6.3 Attendances at football matches[1]
England and Wales, and Scotland (thousands)

	England and Wales				*Scotland*
	Division 1	*Division 2*	*Division 3*	*Division 4*	
1961–62	12 061	7 453	5 199	3 267	3 988
1966–67	14 243	7 254	4 421	2 985	3 242
1971–72	14 485	6 769	4 697	2 749	4 521
1976–77	13 648	6 251	4 152	2 132	2 977
1979–80	12 163	6 112	3 999	2 350	3 381
1980–81	11 393	5 175	3 638	1 701	2 871
1981–82	10 421	4 750	2 837	1 999	2 844

[1] League matches only.
Source: Football League; Scottish Football League.

2 Using the information in Table 6.4* construct

(a) component bar charts; and
(b) pie charts

which show the number of deaths from fire, and their location, during the two years 1971, and 1980. Each year should be represented by the two different types of chart.

Table 6.4 Casualties from fires: by location and cause
United Kingdom (numbers and percentages)

	Fatal				*Non-fatal*			
	1971	*1976*	*1979*	*1980*	*1971*	*1976*	*1979*	*1980*
Location of fire (number of casualties)								
Dwellings	574	690	865	822	3040	3830	6075	6106
Other occupied buildings	152	84	89	104	1 292	1 494	1 889	1 721
Road vehicles	54	60	68	58	187	261	361	282
Other locations	42	61	74	51	498	809	558	665
Total	822	895	1 096	1 035	5 017	6 394	8 883	8 774
Casualties from fires in dwellings caused by (%)								
Smokers, materials and matches	24	25	31	28	14	16	21	20
Space heating	25	24	23	20	23	17	17	15
Malicious or doubtful reasons	4	5	7	9	2	6	8	9
Cooking appliances	3	5	5	5	28	26	24	27
Electric blanket	4	4	5	5	2	3	3	3
Children with fire	6	3	3	4	7	6	6	6
Other causes	10	10	10	10	12	14	13	12
Unknown	25	24	15	19	12	12	8	8
Total (=100%) (numbers)	574	690	865	822	3040	3830	6075	6106

Source: Home Office.

* From *Social Trends*, 1983 (HMSO).

3 Using the information in Table 6.2, which is given in the worked example, construct percentage component bar charts which show the total imports and exports from the regions of England.

4 Refill plc owns over 1000 petrol service stations, and the total annual income from the various sales activities at the service stations is given below. Also shown is the budgeted (predicted) annual income from the sales.

	Sales (£m)	
	Actual	*Budgeted*
Petrol	54.0	50.0
Diesel	9.8	10.0
Accessories	7.2	8.0
Confectionery	4.5	5.0
Car wash	3.6	3.0

Construct an appropriate diagram to represent this information. Your diagram should allow a comparison to be made between the actual and the budgeted sales.

5 A survey of the types of vehicles using a toll bridge in a one hour period produced the following results:

C	C	L	C	B	C	C	C	M	L
B	L	C	L	L	C	C	B	L	L
M	M	M	M	L	C	C	L	C	C
C	C	B	C	C	C	L	M	L	M
C	C	L	C	C	C	C	C	L	C
L	L	C	L	L	L	M	C	C	B
C	L	C	L	M	C	B	C	C	L

C = car; B = bus; L = commercial vehicle; M = motor cycle.

You are required to construct a table which shows the percentage frequency of the different types of vehicle, and to present the information in the form of a pie chart.

7 Graphs and scatter diagrams

7.1 Introduction

Graphs are another method of presenting information; and they are frequently used in presenting business data. The main reason for using graphs is to show the relationship between two variables such as demand for a product and its price, or the cost of production and output. One of the most common variables which is used is *time*: we often see graphs which show profits over time or sales over time.

Graphs tend to highlight the relationship between variables much better than raw data or even tables, and the following example illustrates how useful graphical presentation can be.

The data relates to inland energy consumption in the UK. The first part of the example shows the statistics in tabular form, Table 7.1*, and the same information is then shown in a graph, Figure 7.1.

Table 7.1 Total [unadjusted] inland energy consumption: primary fuel input basis
(million tonnes oil equivalent)

1979		*1980*		*1981*		*1982*	
January	19.3	January	19.1	January	16.6	January	17.3
February	20.4	February	17.9	February	17.2	February	17.1
March	23.6	March	21.8	March	20.3	March	20.2
April	16.6	April	14.9	April	14.1	April	13.8
May	15.3	May	13.9	May	13.4	May	12.7
June	16.9	June	15.7	June	15.0	June	14.7
July	12.3	July	12.1	July	11.5	July	11.2
August	12.5	August	11.0	August	10.6	August	10.7
September	17.2	September	15.4	September	15.1	September	15.3
October	15.3	October	14.8	October	14.8	October	14.0
November	17.9	November	16.2	November	16.1	November	15.3
December	22.0	December	21.6	December	22.1		

From Figure 7.1 it is easy to see that the consumption of fuel follows a very regular monthly pattern. Not only does the graph make the pattern in consumption apparent but it also shows quite clearly that the lowest consumption always occurs in July and August; and that there are two peaks in consumption in March and November. Although the

* From *Monthly Digest of Statistics*, January 1983 (HMSO).

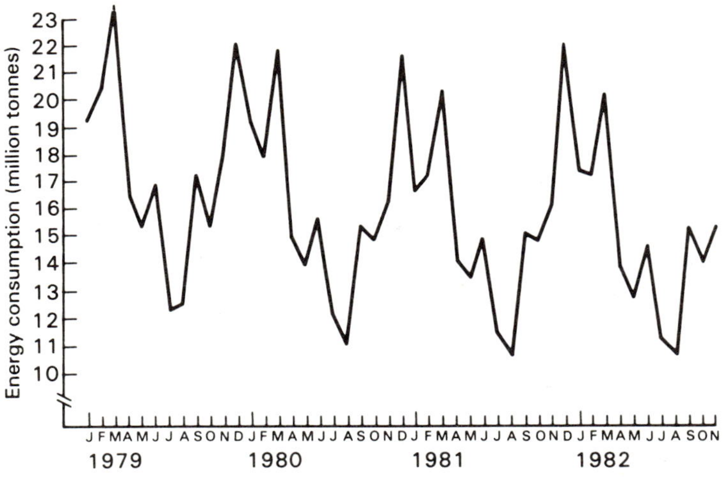

Figure 7.1 Inland energy consumption: primary fuel input basis

pattern of consumption is very definite and clearly shown in the graph it is not easy to perceive it in the table.

7.2 How to construct a graph

The construction of a graph of a simple function is explained in Chapter 4 on equations. The main points to remember are:

(a) There are two axes: x-axis and y-axis. The x-axis is the horizontal axis or *abscissa*, and the y-axis is the vertical axis or *ordinate*.
(b) The point at which the two axes intersect is called the origin and is denoted by 0.
(c) Each axis has a scale. As we shall see the selection of the scale is important because an inappropriate scale might mean that all the data are not shown on the graph, or that the graph gives a misleading impression.
(d) The independent variable (see section 7.7) should be plotted on the x-axis, and the dependent variable on the y-axis.
(e) The units of each variable should be shown.
(f) The scales should be shown.
(g) Sometimes part of the axis can be cut off so that the data can be accommodated within the diagram. If this is done then it should be clearly indicated.
(h) If more than one relationship is included in the graph then each one should be clearly labelled.
(i) The graph should be given a title.

(j) Where it is appropriate the source of the data and any explanatory footnotes should be included in the diagram.

The worked example on page 69 illustrates these main features.

7.3 Choice of scale

The selection of an appropriate scale is important for two reasons.

Firstly selection of an inadequate scale can mean that it is not possible to include all the data on the graph; for example, if the scale on the vertical axis in the worked example only allowed the information to range from 0 to 2 million then the total unemployed after November 1980 could not be shown.

Secondly some scales can give a misleading impression. For example, when the vertical scale is reduced or the horizontal scale elongated then changes in the relationship will seem to be less pronounced – i.e. the slope of any curve or line on the graph becomes less. The opposite is true: when the vertical scale is increased or the horizontal scale reduced then the slope of the curve or line is increased.

Exercise 7.3

(*a*) Using the information included in the graph in the worked example (page 69) explain what would happen to the slope of the curve if
(i) the vertical scale were reduced;
(ii) the horizontal scale were reduced.

(*b*) Using the information given in Table 7.2 construct a graph which shows the unemployed in the distributive trades from May 1978 to May 1982, and compare your graph with the graph in the worked example which shows the total unemployed over the same period.

*Worked example**

Using the information given in Table 7.2 construct a graph which shows the total unemployed from May 1978 to May 1982. The answer is shown in Figure 7.2 on page 69.

7.4 Interpretation of graphs

One of the main reasons why graphs are used to present information is that they convey, in a way which is easy to understand, the relationship between variables.

The first rule in interpretation is to check how the graph has been

* From *Monthly Digest of Statistics*, January 1983 (HMSO).

Table 7.2 Unemployed, excluding school-leavers, industrial analysis, Great Britain (thousands)

	Total unemployed	*Agriculture, forestry and fishing*	*Mining and quarrying*	*Manufacturing*	*Construction*	*Gas, electricity and water*	*Transport and communication*	*Distributive trades*	*Financial, professional and miscellaneous services*	*Public administration and defence*	*Others not classified by industry*
Order in Standard Industrial Classification		I	II	III-XIX	XX	XXI	XXII	XXIII	XXIV–XXVI	XXVII	
Unadjusted											
1978 May	1280	24	22	334	186	9	58	133	219	76	219
August	1324	22	24	337	168	9	55	133	218	76	281
November	1278	23	24	318	166	8	56	126	237	78	241
1979 February	1351	27	25	331	205	9	61	138	242	80	233
May	1202	22	23	314	160	8	54	123	209	72	217
August	1211	20	24	311	139	7	51	122	209	70	258
November	1247	21	25	318	152	7	55	125	240	75	229
1980 February	1387	25	25	365	193	8	64	147	258	77	225
May	1396	23	25	400	190	8	63	147	245	77	219
August	1661	25	26	481	210	8	69	169	279	82	313
November	1968	32	29	593	274	9	85	193	353	95	306
1981 February	2280	40	31	700	349	9	103	229	397	102	321
May	2364	38	32	755	357	10	106	238	396	105	327
August	2564	38	34	799	357	11	109	255	425	113	423
1982 May	2738	43	38	811	366	14	122	286	478	131	450

Answer

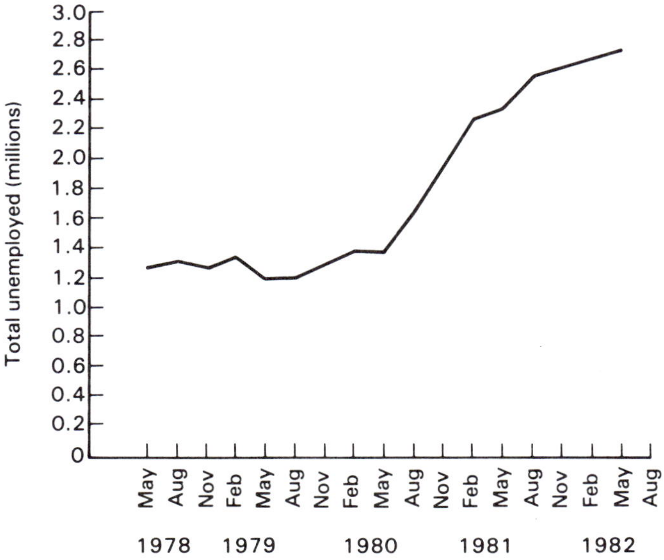

Figure 7.2 Unemployed, excluding school-leavers, Great Britain

constructed: bear in mind that information can be distorted by the use of an inappropriate scale, or the information could be incomplete because the units or the scale are not shown. It is reasonable – but not always essential – when interpreting a graph to support the conclusions with additional business information.

Figures 7.3–7.5 are all taken from government publications* and show how professional statisticians present graphs and interpret them for the general public. An interesting point to note is that in all three examples the vertical scale is shown at the right-hand side of the graph so that recent years can be read more easily.

During 1980 there was a large increase in manual workers in manufacturing industries working short-time, and a corresponding decrease in those working overtime (Figure 7.3). Short-time working reached a peak in January 1981, coinciding with the trough in those working overtime: 594 000 were then on short-time, and 990 000 were working overtime. Since then the situation has improved, and by July 1982 only 86 000 were on short-time. This amounted to 2.3 % of all manual workers in manufacturing industries, compared with 13.7 % in January 1981.

Gas increased its share of all domestic fuel consumption from 40 % in 1975 to 56 % in 1981. Over the same period the percentage shares of all

* All are from *Social Trends*, 1983 (HMSO).

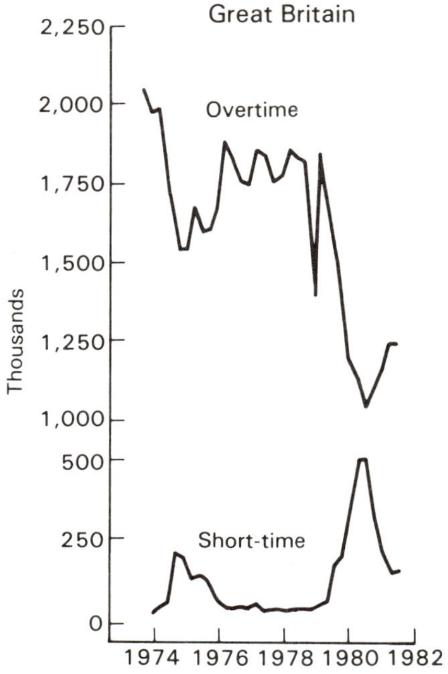

Figure 7.3 Manual workers in manufacturing industries working short-time and overtime

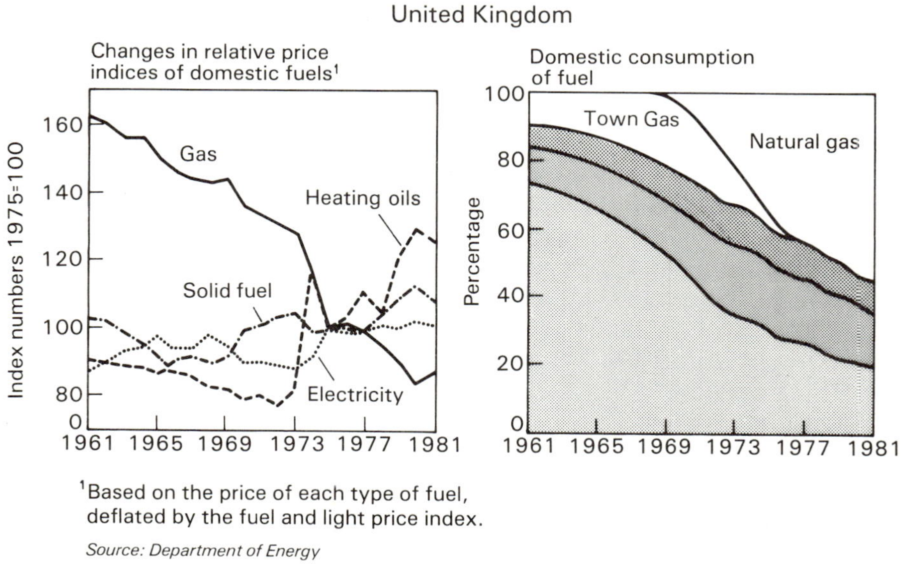

Figure 7.4 Domestic fuels: relative price indices and consumption

the other fuels fell: solid fuel consumed fell from 29 to 20 %; electricity from 21 to 18 %; and heating oils from 10 to 6 %. The change in the proportions consumed is probably a reflection of the changes in the relative prices. Gas was the only fuel where the percentage share of consumption was higher in 1981 than in 1980, even though its relative price increased.

The changing real values (i.e. after allowing for inflation) of unemployment benefit and retirement pension to married couples are illustrated in Figure 7.5. The continuous parts of the lines show the upratings in the level of benefits, while the dotted lines between each uprating represent the erosion of purchasing power by price inflation.

From April 1975 to November 1980 each uprating increased the real value of the state retirement pension. Thus, in November 1980 the retirement pension for a married couple was worth £4.87 more (at April 1982 prices) than it was in April 1975. However, the uprating in November 1981 was below the rate of inflation: the real value of retirement pensions (again at April 1982 prices) was £1.36 less in November 1981 than in November 1980.

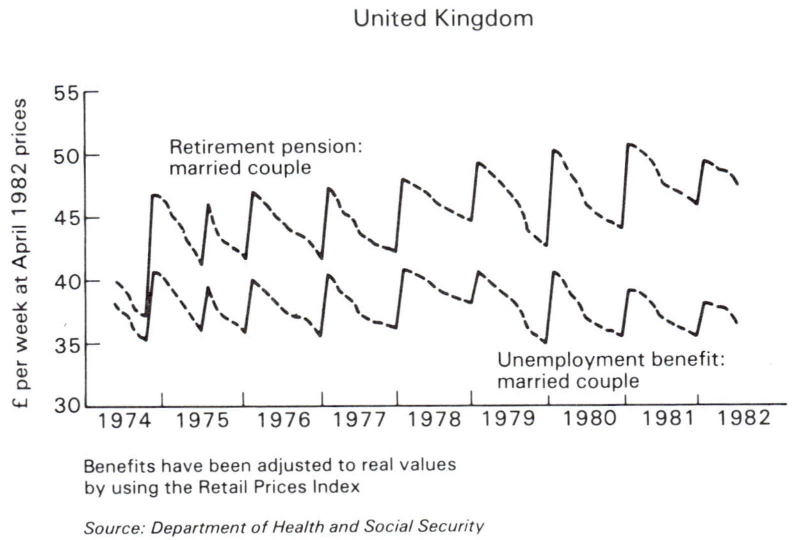

Figure 7.5 Real value of unemployment benefit and retirement pension

The upratings in unemployment benefit more or less maintained its real value between 1974 and 1979. But the last two upratings in November 1980 and 1981 were both less than the inflation rate, with the result that the real value of unemployment benefit (at April 1982 prices) was £2.36 less in November 1981 than in November 1979.

7.5 Semi-logarithmic graphs

The examples which have been given in the chapter so far have shown graphs which deal with absolute changes in the variables. However, if we want to show relative changes, then semi-logarithmic graphs should be used.

The logarithms of a series of numbers give the rate of change in the numbers. Thus if data is converted to logarithms and then plotted against a variable such as time the graph which results shows the rate of growth or decline of the data. For example, if a firm wants to show on a graph the rate of growth of sales over a period of time, it should convert the actual value of the sales to logarithmic values, and then plot the log values on the vertical axis and time on the horizontal axis.

Thus those graphs that show one of the variables in log values are known as semi-logarithmic graphs or ratio scale graphs. It is often more convenient to plot the actual value directly onto graph paper without first converting them to logs. For this purpose special semi-log graph paper can be used; this is graph paper which is marked along the vertical axis in a logarithmic scale, and the horizontal scale is the normal arithmetic scale.

The following example illustrates the use of semi-logarithmic graphs. Table 7.3 shows the value of monthly sales (£thousand) in three divisions of a motor vehicle manufacturer during one trading year. You are required to compare the performance of each division using semi-log graphs.

Table 7.3 (£ thousand)

		Monthly sales	
	A	*B*	*C*
January	2 000	2 000	25 000
February	2 250	2 040	23 750
March	2 500	2 122	22 562
April	2 750	2 249	21 434
May	3 000	2 429	20 362
June	3 250	2 672	19 344
July	3 500	2 993	18 377
August	3 750	3 412	17 458
September	4 000	3 958	16 585
October	4 250	4 670	15 756
November	4 500	5 604	14 968
December	4 750	6 837	14 220

Figure 7.6 enables us to judge the rate of change of each division. By examination of the slope of each line we can see that the growth of sales of division A are increasing at a decreasing rate; B's sales are increasing at an increasing rate; and the rate of C's sales shows a steady decrease.

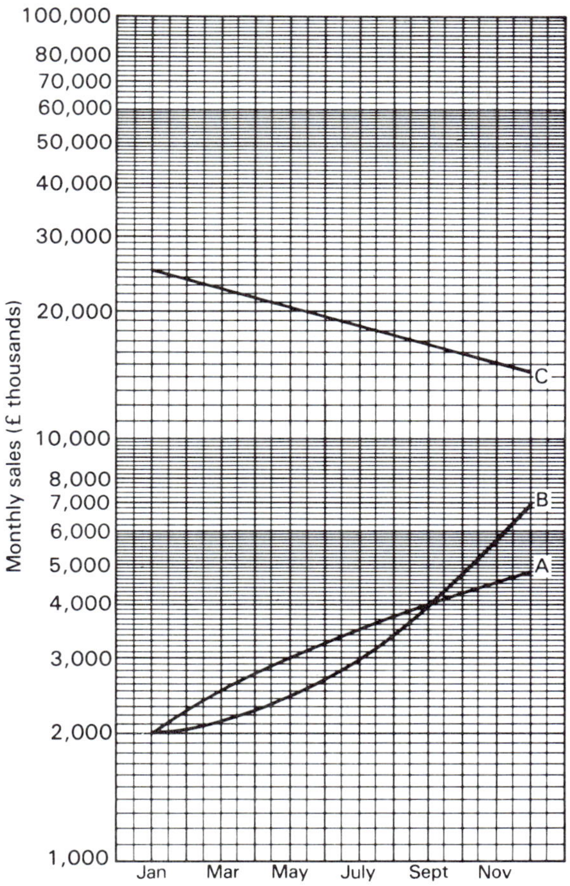

Figure 7.6

7.6 Interpretation of semi-logarithmic graphs

The following are the main features of semi-logarithmic graphs:

(1) Zero and negative variables cannot be shown. The origin cannot start at 0 – log of 0 does not exist – it starts at 1 since the log of 1 is 0.
(2) Semi-log graphs are concerned with the relative change in variables, not the absolute value of the variables, and so variables of very different magnitude can be compared. For example, the rate of change of a small firm's profits can be compared with the aggregate profits of the industry.
(3) Similarly, completely different variables can be compared on the same graph; for example, total output with total unemployment in the UK.

The most important feature of a semi-log graph is the direction of the line on the graph, and Figure 7.7* not only shows the rate of change of usage of the fuels in the UK, but it also includes a key which indicates the value of the rate of change.

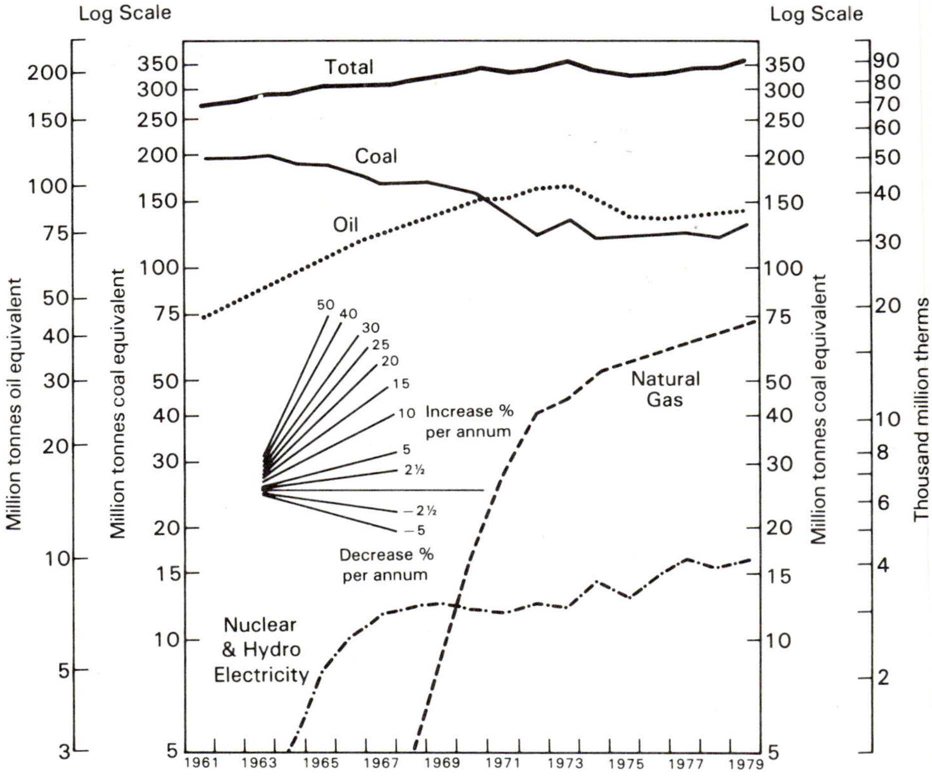

Figure 7.7 Total inland consumption of primary fuels for energy use

7.7 Dependent and independent variables

We have seen in section 7.2 that in order to construct a graph we have to examine the data and decide which of the two variables is the independent variable. The independent variable is always shown on the x-axis; and the dependent variable is plotted on the y-axis.

The *independent variable* (*x*) is the variable which is not, or does not appear to be, dependent on the other variable. For example, time is always the independent variable: time is never dependent on other factors. Another example of an independent variable is fertiliser when it

* From *Digest of UK Energy Statistics*, 1980 (HMSO).

is applied to crops. When a farmer applies a fertiliser to the soil he expects an increase in the yield of his crops; thus the yield is dependent on the amount of fertiliser which is applied, and therefore fertiliser is the independent variable.

It is wrong to assume that because a variable appears to be dependent on another variable that the independent variable actually causes a change in the other. For example, we cannot say categorically that smoking cigarettes causes lung cancer; we can say that there appears to be a relationship between the two, and that the incidence in lung cancer appears to be associated with the smoking of cigarettes.

In some instances it is not always clear which of the two variables is the independent one. For example, if the ages of a husband and wife are plotted against one another, it is difficult to decide which of the variables is independent. In cases such as this either of the variables can be plotted on the x-axis.

7.8 Scatter diagrams

The notion of the dependent and independent variable is important when we try to assess the relationship between variables. There are many examples where two different variables appear to be associated, and it is useful to express such relationships in the form of a scatter diagram. A scatter diagram helps us to assess the strength of the relationship between variables.

For example, a firm wishes to examine the relationship between the money it spends on advertising a particular product and the product's total sales. Table 7.4 shows the advertising expenditure and the total sales for each quarter during a three-year period in £thousand.

Table 7.4 (£ thousand)

	Year 1				*Year 2*				*Year 3*			
	I	II	III	IV	I	II	III	IV	I	II	III	IV
Advertising	12	14	16	18	20	22	24	26	28	30	32	34
Sales	135	130	152	218	205	225	247	250	280	318	342	340

We can assume that if a relationship exists, then sales are dependent on advertising expenditure. So advertising expenditure is the independent variable. Using the data given in the table above we get the scatter diagram shown in Figure 7.8:

From Figure 7.8 it can be seen that an increase in advertising expenditure is accompanied by an increase in sales. The co-ordinates almost give a straight-line relationship, but they do not lie on a line exactly. This is because other variables exist that can influence the firm's

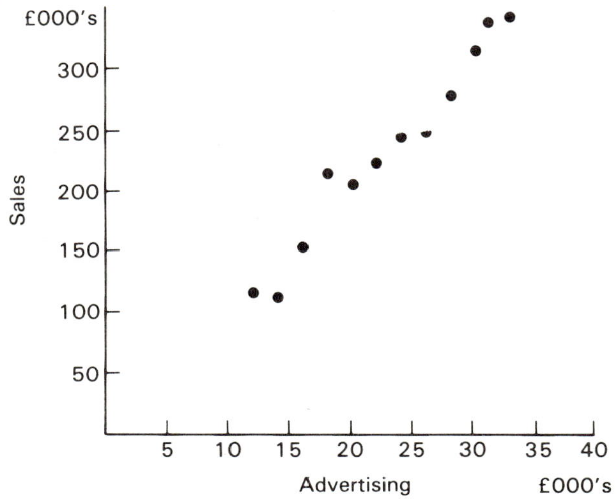

Figure 7.8

sales; for example the price of the product, the price of competitive products, the extent and nature of competitors' advertising, the level of disposable incomes and other general economic conditions.

All of these factors, and many others, will influence the relationship between advertising expenditure and sales; nevertheless by using a statistical technique known as *line of best fit*, it is possible to predict the probable sales from any given amount of expenditure on advertising.

The closer the points are to the line, then the stronger is the degree of relationship between the variables. If the relationship is weak then the points will be widely scattered.

7.9 Different types of relationship

If an increase in one variable is accompanied by an increase in the other variable then they are related *directly*, i.e. there is a positive correlation between the variables. Conversely, where an increase in one variable is associated with a decrease in the other they are related *inversely*, i.e. there is a negative correlation between the variables.

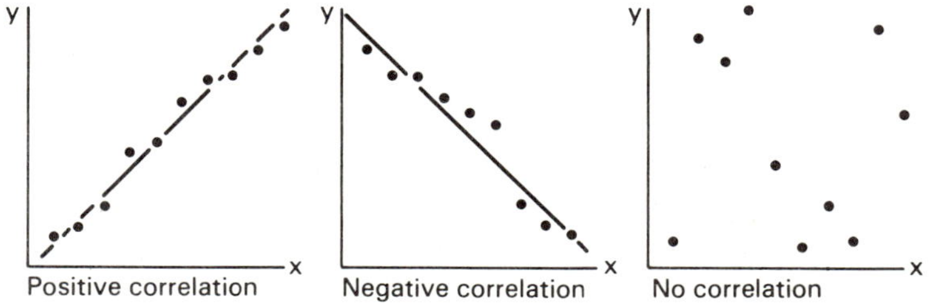

When the points lie approximately on a straight line then a linear relationship exists between the two variables. Where the points approximate to a curve the relationship is curvilinear. There are techniques of curve fitting from which the equation of the curve can be determined.

7.10 Estimating from a line of best fit

Great care should be taken when the line of best fit is used to estimate the likely value of one variable from the value of another. The stronger the degree of relationship then the more accurate the estimate is likely to be. If the relationship is weak – i.e. the points are widely scattered – then you should not have too much confidence in any estimated values.

Estimates should be made only within the limits of the original data. It is most unwise to extrapolate beyond the limits since any relationship between the variable could change.

Additional exercises

1 Using Table 7.5* construct a graph which shows the value of new orders obtained by contractors in each quarter for new housing in the public sector and the total of other new work from the public sector for the four years 1978 to 1981.

2 The figures given in Table 7.6** show the total value of output of the construction industry in the UK, and the total public expenditure from 1965 to 1975.

(a) Construct a scatter diagram of the data.
(b) State whether the variables are directly or inversely related.
(c) Comment on the graph.

3 Using the information in Table 7.7*** draw a semi-logarithmic graph of the use of public service vehicles and private transport vehicles from 1961 to 1981. Comment on your results.

4 Table 7.8 shows the growth of a manufacturing organisation over a five-year period. Plot the two series on the same diagram using semi-logarithmic graph paper to show their relative movements. Comment on the result.

* From *Monthly Digest of Statistics*, January 1983 (HMSO).
** From *Annual Abstract of Statistics*, various (HMSO).
*** From *Social Trends*, 1983 (HMSO).

Table 7.5 Value of new orders obtained by contractors (analysis by type of work)

Great Britain (£ million)

		New housing from public sector	Other new work from public sector: Total	Public authorities: Total	Education: Schools	Education: Universities	Health	Offices, factories, etc.	Roads	Harbours	Water	Sewerage	Miscellaneous	Gas electricity and coal mining	Railways and air transport
1977		1173	2298	1848	251	24	202	327	392	98	96	142	316	330	121
1978		1271	2677	2251	231	26	261	585	424	107	79	184	354	306	121
1979		1056	2991	2551	305	26	287	582	466	111	82	196	497	362	78
1980		758	3394	2680	292	38	320	589	562	97	67	227	487	541	173
1981		872	3750	2983	239	42	478	519	781	95	129	211	489	492	275
1978	1st qr	328	618	538	59	7	56	174	89	16	26	44	68	64	17
	2nd qr	373	614	503	95	8	47	113	71	27	17	42	83	68	41
	3rd qr	303	726	618	44	5	84	163	135	26	18	47	96	81	27
	4th qr	268	720	592	33	6	74	135	129	38	19	51	107	93	36
1979	1st qr	272	761	632	77	3	64	142	131	20	17	51	127	112	17
	2nd qr	304	860	748	145	9	67	176	128	22	23	49	127	91	21
	3rd qr	259	709	616	53	4	99	136	99	32	28	52	113	72	21
	4th qr	222	661	555	29	9	57	127	108	37	14	44	130	87	18
1980	1st qr	235	847	659	73	15	88	143	129	12	17	55	125	135	53
	2nd qr	202	903	813	137	7	90	140	145	32	23	56	184	57	33
	3rd qr	196	837	693	48	9	68	156	214	26	22	61	90	109	34
	4th qr	126	808	515	34	7	75	150	74	27	5	55	88	240	53
1981	1st qr	153	998	712	70	6	117	179	101	36	27	38	139	224	62
	2nd qr	156	1112	851	82	14	81	109	301	23	41	56	144	94	167
	3rd qr	160	868	727	47	11	159	117	185	21	50	58	79	119	23
	4th qr	204	771	692	40	11	121	114	194	15	12	59	126	55	23

Table 7.6 Public expenditure and output in the construction industry, UK, 1965–75 (£ million)

	1965	*1966*	*1967*	*1968*	*1969*	*1970*	*1971*	*1972*	*1973*	*1974*	*1975*
Construction industry– total value of output	4 118	4 375	4 680	5 077	5 257	5 577	6 182	7 021	8 996	10 188	11 610
Total public expenditure	12 681	13 764	15 809	17 199	17 729	19 721	22 114	24 955	29 363	38 093	49 952

Table 7.7 Passenger transport: use and prices, Great Britain
(thousand million passenger kilometres and price indices)

	1961	*1966*	*1971*	*1975*	*1976*	*1979*	*1980*	*1981*
Use (thousand million passenger kilometres)								
Air[1]	1.0	1.8	2.0	2.2	2.3	2.8	2.8	2.6
Rail[2]	39	35	36	35	33	36	36	35
Road								
Public service vehicles	69	62	56	54	53	52	51	49
Private transport[3]	161	255	330	352	367	405	423	422
Bicycles	11	7	5	4	4	4	5	5
Total	281	361	429	447	459	500	518	514
Price indices (1975 = 100)								
Implied cost to the consumer[4] of:								
Air fares		58	62	100	118	153	181	191
Railway fares	31	40	57	100	129	184	225	246
Bus and coach stage service fares	30	40	61	100	125	189	240	269
New and second-hand cars and motorcycles	56	48	61	100	119	207	237	250
Motor-vehicle running costs	35	41	53	100	111	158	193	224
All transport and travel	40	44	58	100	116	176	208	231
Retail Prices Index (all items)	38	45	59	100	117	166	196	219

[1] Domestic scheduled journeys only, including Northern Ireland and the Channel Isles.
[2] British Railways, plus London Transport and Glasgow underground railways, and other railways.
[3] Based on statistics of vehicle-kilometres derived from traffic counts and estimates of average number of persons per vehicle derived from the Motoring and National Travel Surveys.
[4] Based on national accounts estimates of consumers' expenditure.
Source: Department of Transport, Central Statistical Office.

Table 7.8 Growth of a manufacturing firm over a five-year period
(£ thousand)

	Year 1	*Year 2*	*Year 3*	*Year 4*	*Year 5*
Turnover	140	800	2400	3600	8200
Cost of materials	60	320	1000	1500	2800

5 Table 7.9 gives the tonnage and the service speed of the passenger liners of RINK LTD. a shipping company:

Table 7.9 Tonnage and service speed of the passenger liners of Rink Ltd

Gross tonnage	*Service speed (knots)*
26 000	25.0
21 700	24.0
26 000	25.0
21 630	24.0
20 300	19.4
15 020	21.6
15 010	21.6
20 100	20.0
26 300	24.6
21 660	20.5
10 470	19.4
20 450	22.2
11 730	20.1
12 150	19.9
16 990	19.6
19 930	19.4
14 440	19.0
9 420	19.3

Using the data construct a scatter diagram and comment on the result.

8 Averages

8.1 Discrete and continuous data

Discrete data is data which occurs only as *whole numbers* (*integers*). For example people, objects, goods, equipment, or anything which can be distinctly counted in individual items is discrete data. Thus, if we are conducting a survey into the number of people in employment or the number of accidents in a locality, then each item of data can only exist as a whole number, i.e. 4 people or 67 people and so on.

Data which occurs over a range of values – and not simply as whole numbers – is called *continuous data.* So any measurement of such variables as weight, height, length, time, temperature is continuous: material can be cut into lengths of 35 cm or 35.001 cm; time can be divided into days, hours, minutes, seconds and so on. Obviously there are limits to the degree of accuracy to which things can be measured; nevertheless the measuring process gives a range of values on a continuous not discrete scale.

8.2 Purpose of averages

An average is a single statistic which is used to represent a series of figures. Its purpose is to give a value which is typical of the data, and very often this value is in the middle of the series and consequently an average is often referred to as a measure of central tendency.

For example, if we learn that average earnings in the UK are £6 000 per annum and in Germany they are £7 000 then we could assume that, on the whole, a German tends to earn more than a worker in the UK. We should realise, of course, that an average is an indication of tendency and that many in the UK will earn more than some Germans.

There are many ways in which a series of figures can occur, and consequently there are several types of average which can be used. Three important averages which are used in business are the *arithmetic mean*, the *median* and the *mode.*

8.3 The arithmetic mean

The arithmetic mean is the average. It is calculated by adding up the values of the variables and then dividing by the number of variables; so that, in cricket, a batsman who has three innings and scores 25, 78 and 6 would have a mean average score of 109 ÷ 3 = 33 runs.

Example 8.3a

A small firm employs 7 operatives, and the following shows the number of days each employee was absent from work during a 3-month period. Calculate the mean number of days lost through absence.

Employee	A	B	C	D	E	F	G
Days absent	2	4	10	7	5	12	6

$$\text{Arithmetic mean} = \frac{2+4+10+7+5+12+6}{7} = \frac{46}{7} = 6.57 \text{ days}$$

In general the formula for the arithmetic mean of *n* numbers is:

$$\text{AM} = \frac{X_1 + X_2 + X_3 + \ldots + X_n}{n}$$

where *X* represents the value of each variable and *n* is the number of variables.

The formula for the arithmetic mean requires the values of the variables to be added. This *summation* process is denoted by the sign sigma Σ. Using the sign sigma the above formula can be written as:

$$\text{AM} = \frac{\sum_{i=1}^{n} x_i}{n}$$

$\sum_{i=1}^{n} x_i$ means the 'sum of' *n* values of *x*. The first value is represented by x_1, the second by x_2, etc., and the last number by x_n.

Example 8.3b

Calculate the mean for the data in Table 8.1.

Table 8.1 UK Inland Energy Consumption, 1969–79

(million therms)

1969	*1970*	*1971*	*1972*	*1973*	*1974*	*1975*	*1976*	*1977*	*1978*	*1979*
81 992	84 146	82 741	84 432	88 301	83 839	80 421	81 709	83 680	84 020	87 814

When, as in this example, we have to find the mean of data which includes large numbers it is helpful to subtract a constant from each item to make the figures more manageable. (In this instance we shall subtract 80 000.) The mean can be calculated on the easier figures, and the constant is then added. Thus we get:

$$1992+4146+2741+4432+8301+3839+421+1709 \\ +3680+4020+7814=43\,095$$

$$\text{The mean is } \frac{43\,095}{11}+80\,000=83\,918 \text{ million therms.}$$

In some series the same values can occur several times. For example the following is a list of the marks which 34 students were given for an assignment:

4, 4   5, 5, 5   6   7, 7, 7   8, 8, 8, 8, 8   9, 9, 9, 9, 9, 9
10, 10, 10, 10, 10   11, 11   12, 12   13, 13, 13   14   15

Instead of adding each item individually the mean can be calculated in the following way:

$$\frac{2(4)+3(5)+6+3(7)+\ldots+2(12)+3(13)+14+15}{34}$$

This will give:

$$\frac{8+15+6+21+40+54+50+22+24+39+14+15}{34}$$

which gives an average mark of 9.06.

The number of times a variable occurs is referred to as its *frequency* (frequency of occurrence). We can see from this example that, where a variable occurs several times, it can be multiplied by its frequency; the results are then added together and this addition is then divided by the total number of frequencies.

8.4 Frequency distribution

The variables in most data occur in frequencies, and the following example shows how a frequency distribution is represented, and how a mean is calculated from such a distribution.

Worked example 8.4

In a survey of 1000 families in a rural area the following distribution, which shows the number of children in each family, was obtained. Calculate the mean number of children per family.

No of children (x)	*No of families* (f)	fx
0	114	0
1	215	215
2	356	712
3	189	567
4	97	388
5	24	120
6	5	30
Total	1000	2032

The formula for the arithmetic mean when the data is grouped in this form of frequency distribution is:

$$\bar{x} = \frac{\Sigma fx}{\Sigma f}$$

where $\bar{x}$ is the arithmetic mean;
Σfx is the sum of the fx column; and
Σf is the sum of the frequencies (f).

Using the formula we get $\bar{x} = \dfrac{2032}{1000}$

$\bar{x} = 2.032$ children

8.5 Grouped frequency distribution

In some instances there can be a large number of items in the data; and, as we saw on pages 45 and 46, such data is often grouped into classes. The following example uses the grouped frequency distribution which is given on page 46, and illustrates how the arithmetic mean is calculated from grouped data.

Worked example 8.5

Calculate the mean height of policemen from the grouped distribution on page 46.

The first step is to close the open-ended classes by using any appropriate class limits:

Height (cm)	*Height (cm)*	*No of men*
less than 175	170–174	7
	175–179	15
	180–184	18
	185–189	17
more than 189	190–194	3

The next step is to select a height which represents each class. The most appropriate height is the mid-point of the class. We then, as in the previous example, multiply x by f. We now have:

Height (cm) (x)	*No of men* (f)	fx
172	7	1 204
177	15	2 655
182	18	3 276
187	17	3 179
192	3	576
Total	60	10 890

$$\bar{x} = \frac{10890}{60} = 181.5\,\text{cm}$$

Exercise 8.5

Using the raw data on page 45 calculate the arithmetic mean of the height of the policemen, and compare your results with the answer given above in example 5.

8.6 Short-cut method of computing the arithmetic mean

The method given in example 8.5 for calculating the mean is an accurate method; but, if the data are complex or in large numbers then it can be cumbersome. Consequently the formula for the mean has been amended to give a short-cut method of computation. The following example illustrates this shortened method.

Worked example 8.6

Using the information in Table 8.2* calculate the arithmetic mean age of males receiving treatment for drug addiction in 1971.

* From *Social Trends*, 1983 (HMSO).

Table 8.2 Dangerous drugs–notified addicts receiving treatment: by age and sex

United Kingdom (Numbers)

	People receiving treatment aged					
	15–19	*20–24*	*25–29*	*30–34*	*35–49*	*50 or over*
Males						
1971	89	596	214	88	70	64
1976	11	298	658	188	136	92
1979	11	259	770	531	202	109
1980	18	221	705	697	238	110
1981	41	385	883	950	323	114
Females						
1971	29	126	74	24	42	113
1976	7	114	151	62	53	97
1979	23	169	246	141	86	97
1980	16	175	277	155	88	99
1981	43	240	349	235	116	102

Age class	*Mid-point* x	*Frequency* f	d	d/c	$f(d/c)$
15–19	17	89	−10	−2	−178
20–24	22	596	− 5	−1	−596
25–29	27 (*am*)	214	0	0	0
30–34	32	88	+ 5	+1	+ 88
35–49	42	70	+15	+3	+210
50 or over	62	64	+35	+7	+448
		$\Sigma f = 1121$			$\Sigma f(d/c) = -28$

The steps to be followed when applying the short cut method of calculating the arithmetic mean are:

Step 1 List the mid-point of each class (x) and its respective frequency (f).

Step 2 Select the class which is likely to include the mean (in this case 27). This is called the assumed mean (*am*).

Step 3 Calculate how each value of x deviates from the assumed mean (d).

Step 4 Divide each deviation by a common constant $\left(\frac{d}{c}\right)$ (in this case 5).

Step 5 Multiply $\frac{d}{c}$ by $f\left(f\cdot\frac{d}{c}\right)$.

The formula which is then applied is:

$$\text{The arithmetic mean} = am + \frac{c(\Sigma f\cdot d/c)}{n} \quad [n = \Sigma f]$$

Substituting the values from above into the formula we get:

$$\bar{x} = 27.00 + \frac{5(-28)}{1121} = 27.00 - 0.12 = 26.88 \text{ years}$$

Exercise 8.6

Calculate the arithmetic mean in example 8.6 using the long method and compare your answer with the short-cut method answer.

8.7 Advantages and disadvantages of the arithmetic mean

The main advantage of the arithmetic mean is that it is mathematically sound because it uses the actual values in a distribution. It is, therefore, a useful statistic when further or more advanced analysis is required.

A second advantage, of course, is that it is a readily understood statistic.

However, because all values are used in the calculation, then extreme values can distort the mean so that it does not always give a fair representation of a distribution. For instance, in the example on page 82 if one person were absent for the whole of the three months this would exaggerate the average number of days lost. (Include in the figures on page 82 an employee who is absent for 60 days and calculate the new mean, and assess how representative it is.)

A second disadvantage is that the mean may be a number which does not exist in the original data. For instance, in the example on page 84, no family has 2.032 children.

8.8 The median

The median average is a useful alternative to the mean because it is not distorted by extreme values in the data. The median is the value of the variable which lies exactly in the middle of an array of the data when it is arranged in rank order.

Worked example 8.8a

Table 8.3 Number of accidents for every 100 000 people at risk in five industries

Manufacturing	2 900
Construction	3 000
Railways	2 400
Coalmining	15 200
Agriculture	1 400

Calculate and compare the median average and mean average number of accidents for all five industries.

To calculate the median arrange the data in a rank order array: 1400, 2400, 2900, 3000, 15200. The median is the middle value, i.e. 2900 accidents.

$$\text{The arithmetic mean is } \frac{1\,400 + 2\,400 + 2\,900 + 3\,000 + 15\,200}{5}$$

$$= \frac{24\,900}{5} = 4\,980 \text{ accidents}$$

In this example the mean average is not as representative of the data as the median; it is considerably higher than four of the five industries because it has been distorted by the very high level of accidents in coalmining.

A problem occurs in calculating the median when an array contains an even number of variables because one number is not exactly in the middle of the data. In such cases the two middle numbers are selected, and the arithmetic mean of these two values is the median.

Worked example 8.8b

Table 8.4 Number of accidents for every 100 000 people at risk in six industries

Manufacturing	3 300
Construction	3 100
Railways	2 800
Coalmining	16 800
Quarrying	3 400
Agriculture	1 400

To calculate the median we put these values in rank order: 1400, 2800, 3100, 3300, 3400, 16800.

$$\text{The median} = \frac{3100 + 3300}{2} = 3200 \text{ accidents.}$$

8.9 Calculation of the median from a frequency distribution

Even though, in a frequency distribution, we can be dealing with a large number of variables we continue to apply the principle of selecting the value of the variable in the middle of the data.

Example 8.9

The following table shows the height in ascending order of 38 policemen. The median value is the height of the policeman in the middle, i.e. the nineteenth which is 182 cm.

Height (cm)	*No of policemen (frequency)*	*Cumulative number (cumulative frequency)*
177	2	2
178	2	4
179	6	10
181	5	15
182	**4**	**19**
183	2	21
184	7	28
185	5	33
186	5	38
	38	

8.10 Calculation of the median from grouped frequency distribution

Since the median is the value of the variable in the middle of the data, it can be calculated from grouped data using either interpolation or a formula.

Calculation by interpolation

Worked example 8.10

The following grouped frequency table shows the height of 60 policemen. Using the interpolation method, calculate the median.

Height (cm) x	*Frequency* f	*Cumulative frequency* F
170–174	7	7
175–179	15	22
180–184	18	**40**
185–189	17	57
190–194	3	60
	60	

The median is the 60/2 = 30th item, and this is in the group 180–184 cm. Since the sum of the two previous groups is 22 then the median value is the eighth item in the third group. If we assume that the variable is distributed continuously, then the 18 items in the median group are distributed between 179.5 and 184.5 cm; and the median lies 8/18 of way between these two values, i.e. by interpolation the median is:

$$179.5 + 8/18\ (184.5 - 179.5) = 179.5 + 8/18\ (5) = 181.72 \text{ cm}$$

Calculation using the formula

The formula for calculating the median is:

$$Lm + c\left[\frac{N/2 - Fm - 1}{fm}\right]$$

Applying the formula to grouped data in example 8.10 we get:

Lm	= lower class limit of median group	=	179.5;
c	= class width of the median group	=	5.0;
N	= total number of frequencies	=	60.0;
$Fm - 1$	= cumulative frequency before median group	=	22.0;
fm	= frequency of the median group	=	18.0.

Substituting the values into the formula we get:

$$179.5 + 5\left[\frac{60/2 - 22}{18}\right] = 179.5 + 5\,(8/18) = 181.72 \text{ cm}$$

8.11 Advantages and disadvantages of the median

The main advantage of the median is that extreme items do not affect its value; because of this it is considered the most useful average to represent wages in wage negotiation. A second advantage is that when it is found directly it can represent an actual item.

However it can be tedious to arrange the data into an array, and the median has limited application when mathematical analysis of the data is necessary.

8.12 The mode

A third type of average is the mode. The mode is that value which occurs most frequently in a distribution. It is often used when describing different sizes of clothing, so that the average shirt size or average shoe size in a given population is that size which most people wear.

Example 8.12

The following gives the sizes of 15 pairs of running shoes sold in a sports shop during one day's trading. Calculate the mode.

7, 9, 6, 2, 5, 6, 3, 3, 4, 6, 5, 8, 7, 4, 6.

Since size 6 occurs most frequently (four times) then the mode = 6

8.13 Bimodal data

It is likely, in some distributions, that different values will occur with the same frequency. In these cases the distribution is described as bimodal. Thus, in Example 8.12, if two extra size 4 shoes had been sold then the data would have had two modes: 4 and 6.

There are cases, for instance in example 8.8b on page 88, where each variable occurs only once. In such cases the data does not have a mode.

8.14 The mode of a frequency distribution

The mode is the variable which occurs most often. So if we examine the data on page 89 which shows the height of 38 policemen we can see that 184 cm occurs more than any other height (7 times); therefore 184 cm is the mode.

8.15 The mode of a grouped frequency distribution

By definition the mode is the variable with the highest frequency; therefore, as we have seen in section 8.14, in a frequency distribution the mode is easy to determine. However, when the frequencies are grouped it becomes more difficult to calculate the mode.

The solution is to apply a formula; by taking the class with the highest frequency, and using the frequencies before and after this class we can estimate which variable is the mode.

Worked example 8.15

Using the grouped frequency distribution given in Table 8.5, which is taken from Table 8.2, calculate the mode.

Table 8.5 Male addicts receiving treatment for dangerous drugs, 1971

Age (yrs)	*Frequency (f)*	
15–19	89	f_{m-1}
20–24	596	f_m
25–29	214	f_{m+1}
30–34	88	
35–49	70	
50 +	64	

The method for calculating the mode is as follows:

Step 1 Decide which class contains the mode: this is the class with the highest frequency. In this example the mode lies in the range 20–24 years (or more accurately 19.5–24.5 years).

Step 2 Apply the following formula to the modal group:

$$\text{Mode} = L_{\text{mode}} + \left[\frac{\Delta_1}{\Delta_1 + \Delta_2}\right] C$$

L_{mode} = lower class limit of modal group = 19.5;
$\Delta_1 = f_m - f_{m-1}$, i.e. the difference between the frequencies of the modal class and the class below = 507;
$\Delta_2 = f_m - f_{m+1}$, i.e. the difference between the frequencies of the modal class and the class above = 382;
C = class width = 5.

Applying the formula,

$$\text{the mode} = 19.5 + \left[\frac{507}{507 + 382}\right] 5$$

$$= 19.5 + \left(\frac{507}{889}\right) \times 5 = 19.5 + 2.85 = 22.35$$

The mode is 22.4 years.

8.16 Advantages and disadvantages of the mode

The mode, unlike the mean, is not distorted by extreme values in the data. It is simply the variable which occurs most in a distribution, and as such it is a useful measure of demand or popularity. For example, in the retail trade, where many items are sold in different sizes or colours, the mode is a measure of the most popular type sold, and indicates which items should be kept in stock. Similarly, if machines or equipment have to be designed for use by the average person, then the most appropriate average to use is the mode.

However, the mode is not a sophisticated measure; it does not use all the data in a distribution, and therefore it is not a suitable statistic to use in further analysis of the data.

Additional exercises

1 The following table gives the inland consumption of fuels in the UK from the first quarter of 1978 to the third quarter of 1981 in million tonnes of coal or coal equivalent.

	1st qtr	*2nd qtr*	*3rd qtr*	*4th qtr*
1978	98.0	79.8	69.1	92.9
1979	107.7	83.0	71.2	93.7
1980	99.9	75.7	65.4	89.6
1981	91.8	72.4	63.2	

Calculate (a) the arithmetic mean; and (b) the median of the quarterly consumption of fuels.

2 The following figures give the expenditure (in £ thousand) in one year on advertising by 48 retail organisations, each of which has an annual turnover of around half a million pounds:

14	12	10	9	3	6	10	12
10	10	4	10	8	10	13	9
15	3	11	6	12	11	9	2
19	16	20	8	9	34	10	15
5	11	11	41	10	11	1	14
20	15	7	9	17	9	12	10

Using the raw data: (a) compile a simple frequency distribution; (b) find the mean, median and mode expenditure on advertising; and (c) comment on the results.

Using the information in Table 8.6*:
(a) Construct two frequency distributions to show:
(i) the age groups; and
(ii) the corresponding frequency of births within each group for the years 1951 and 1980.
(b) Calculate the median age in 1951 and in 1980.
(c) Using your answers to (a) and (b), comment on the changes in the distribution of live births in the two years.

Table 8.6 Live births: totals and rates
Great Britain (thousands and rates)

	Total live births (thousand)	*Crude birth rate*[1]	*General fertility rate*[2]	*Age-specific live birth rates*[3] *per 1000 women aged*						*Total period fertility rate*
				15–19	*20–24*	*25–29*	*30–34*	*35–39*	*40–44*	
1951	768	15.7	72.5	21	126	135	90	47	14	2.16
1956	796	16.0	78.2	27	148	152	90	47	13	2.38
1961	912	17.8	90.0	37	173	178	104	49	14	2.78
1966	946	17.8	91.1	48	177	175	98	46	12	2.78
1971	870	16.1	84.2	51	155	155	78	33	8	2.40
1976	649	11.9	61.0	33	111	120	58	18	4	1.72
1977	632	11.6	58.8	30	105	119	59	18	4	1.68
1978	661	12.2	60.7	30	108	124	64	20	4	1.75
1979	706	13.0	64.1	31	112	133	70	21	5	1.86
1980	725	13.3	64.9	31	114	135	71	22	5	1.89
1981	703	12.9	62.0	29[4]	109[4]	130[4]	69[4]	22[4]	5[4]	1.82

[1] Total births per 1000 population of all ages
[2] Total births per 1000 women aged 15–44 includes also births to mothers aged under 15 and 45 and over
[3] Births to mothers aged under 15 and 45 and over are included in the age groups 15–19 and 40–44 respectively
[4] England & Wales figures estimated from births during March quarter

Source: Office of Population Censuses and Surveys. General Register Office (Scotland).

3 A local government inspector visited a retail outlet and weighed all the stock of two brands of pre-packed sugar, and he produced the following table:

	Mean weight (g)	*Total weight (kg)*
Brand A	996	72.708
Brand B	1007	49.343

Calculate the mean weight of the total stock of sugar.

4 The following frequency distribution gives the value of orders taken by a representative of a publishing firm during one financial year:

* From *Social Trends*, 1983 (HMSO).

Value of orders (£)	*Number of orders*
15–29	85
30–59	120
60–89	225
90–149	135
150–299	105
300 and over	20

You are required to illustrate the data by means of a bar chart. Calculate the median and mark it on the bar chart.

5 In 1984 a random sample of the final accounts of 100 companies in the construction industry gave the following frequency of distribution of profit:

Profit (£m)	*Number of Companies*
−10 and under −5	4
−5 and under 0	0
0 and under 5	4
5 and under 10	8
10 and under 15	16
15 and under 20	22
20 and under 25	26
25 and under 30	12
30 and under 35	8

Calculate the mean profit and the median profit for 1984 and comment on your results.

9 Index numbers

9.1 Introduction

Index numbers, such as the *Financial Times Index* or the *Index of Retail Prices*, are familiar business statistics. They are, in fact, percentages; although it is customary not to show the percentage sign. They provide a useful means of measuring changes – over a period of time – in the price or volume of commodities by expressing the value in one period as a percentage of the value in the other period.

We can, of course, easily calculate actual price or volume changes by subtracting one from the other. However, if we wanted to compare changes in several commodities then the percentage change gives a more accurate basis for comparison than the actual change. The purpose of index numbers is to provide a standard measure of comparison.

9.2 Calculation of an index

Table 9.1 illustrates how an index number is calculated.

Table 9.1 Price changes of a washing machine in four different years

Year	*Price* (£)	*Calculation of index*
1976	150	150/150 × 100 = 100
1978	183	183/150 × 100 = 122
1980	210	210/150 × 100 = 140
1983	240	240/150 × 100 = 160

The table shows that the price of the washing machine increased by 22 % from 1976 to 1978, by 40 % from 1976 to 1980, and by 60 % from 1976 to 1983.

You will see from this calculation that the prices in 1978, 1980 and 1983 have been compared with the price in 1976. The year 1976, in this instance, is called the *base year*, and it is usually written 1976 = 100. The year which is compared with the base year is termed *current year*.

Almost all indices are comparisons over time (the exceptions are educational and sociological indices); and the selection of the base period is the first step in the calculation. The general rule is to select a base period which gives a fair and representative basis for comparison.

9.3 Price relative and quantity relative

A *price relative* measures changes in the price of a single commodity over a period of time; and the index numbers calculated in the example in section 9.2 are examples of price relatives.

Instead of changes in the price of the commodity we may be interested in changes in its quantity or volume, such as the quantity of a commodity sold or the volume of a particular item exported. The index number of a single item using quantities or volumes is called a *quantity relative.*

Example 9.3

The output of a small manufacturing firm fell from 2700 units in 1980 to 2500 units in 1983. Find the quantity relative using 1980 as the base year.

Answer

Base year 1980 (100%) output = 2700 units

Current year 1983 output = 2500 units

$$\text{The quantity relative} = \frac{2500}{2700} \times 100 = 92.59$$

$$= 93 \text{ (to the nearest whole number)}$$

The index number of 93 shows that there was a fall in output of 7% from 1980 to 1983. This illustrates an important point that index numbers can show decreases as well as increases.

9.4 Combining indices

In many instances in business we are interested in changes in the price or volume of several items; in these cases we can calculate an average index or an *all items* index.

In order to combine several items we must indicate their relative importance by assigning a value or weight to each of them. For instance, if we are measuring changes in the cost of living then it would be realistic to give the cost of food a greater weight than the cost of footwear.

Given the price relative or quantity relative of each item and its corresponding weight, then the weighted arithmetic mean of the indices can be calculated to give an average or combined index number.

Example 9.4

Table 9.2 gives the weights and the price indices of the items which are included in the Index of Retail Prices. Using this information the all items index for 1981 is calculated.

Table 9.2 Weights and price indices of items in the Index of Retail Prices.

Item	*Weights (W)*	*Price index (1981) (I)*	*(W × I)*
Food	253	277.5	70 207.5
Alcoholic drink	70	306.1	21 427.0
Tobacco	43	358.2	15 402.6
Housing	124	318.2	39 456.8
Fuel and light	52	380.0	19 760.0
Durable household goods	64	237.2	15 180.8
Clothing and footwear	91	208.3	18 955.3
Transport and vehicles	135	322.6	43 551.0
Miscellaneous goods	63	300.7	18 944.1
Services	54	300.8	16 243.2
Meals outside the home	51	318.0	16 218.0
	1000	1974 = 100	295 346.3

In order to calculate the weighted average the following steps are necessary:

Step 1 List the weight (W) and price index (I) of each item. In this example the weights and price indices are given; however, there are exercises, such as those at the end of this chapter, which require the price index of each item to be calculated.

Step 2 Multiply each item's weighting by its price index ($W \times I$).

Step 3 Find the total of ($W \times I$), and divide it by the total weights.

$$\text{The 1981 all items index} = \frac{\Sigma (W \times I)}{\Sigma W}$$

$$= \frac{295\,346}{1000} = 295.346$$

The weighted average expressed as an index is:

1981 = 295 where 1974 = 100

9.5 Published indices

Because they offer a quick and easy method of comparing changes in prices and volume there are many indices published in business. For example, we are all familiar with the Financial Times Index of Share Prices which is published every day in most newspapers and included in television and radio broadcasts. The reason for its popularity is that it is recognised as an immediate indicator of business reaction to economic and general news.

Some of the most important economic and business indices are produced by government departments; and the following list gives examples:

Agricultural prices
Average earnings
Gross National Product
Imports and exports
Industrial production
Industrial share prices
Output
Retail prices
Tax and prices
Wage rates
Wholesale prices

The most well-known index published by the government is the Index of Retail Prices, which is taken to be a measure of the annual rate of inflation. It is, in fact, an average or combined index which is published every month, and it measures the change in prices of the goods and services purchased by most households in the UK.

The categories of items with their respective weightings, which are included in the Index of Retail Prices, are given in the example in section 9.4. These categories include more than 600 goods and services, for which the price changes are regularly measured in more than 200 centres. The weightings of the items are revised each year using information supplied by the Family Expenditure Survey. The base year for the Index is 1974.

Table 9.3* gives the indices of the main groups used in the Index of Retail Prices from 1974 to 1981; and it shows how the weighting of each group altered during that period.

Exercises

1 From the information given above in the index of retail prices calculate an all items index for 1979 using:

(a) base year weights; and
(b) current year weights (1974 = 100).

2 From the information given above in the Index of Retail Prices use base year weights to calculate an average index for 1981 which measures

* From *Social Trends*, 1983 (HMSO).

Table 9.3 Index of retail price

15 January 1974 = 100

	All items	*Food*	*Alcoholic drink*	*Tobacco*	*Housing*	*Fuel and light*	*Durable household goods*	*Clothing and footwear*	*Transport and vehicles*	*Miscellaneous goods*	*Services*	*Meals bought and consumed outside the home*
Weights												
1974	1000	253	70	43	124	52	64	91	135	63	54	51
1975	1000	232	82	46	108	53	70	89	149	71	52	48
1976	1000	228	81	46	112	56	75	84	140	74	57	47
1977	1000	247	83	46	112	58	63	82	139	71	54	45
1978	1000	233	85	48	113	60	64	80	140	70	56	51
1979	1000	232	77	44	120	59	64	82	143	69	59	51
1980	1000	214	82	40	124	59	69	84	151	74	62	41
1981	1000	207	79	36	135	62	65	81	152	75	66	42
Annual averages												
1974	108.5	106.1	109.7	115.9	105.8	110.7	107.9	109.4	111.0	111.2	106.8	108.2
1975	134.8	133.3	135.2	147.7	125.5	147.4	131.2	125.7	143.9	138.6	135.5	132.4
1976	157.1	159.9	159.3	171.3	143.2	182.4	144.2	139.4	166.0	161.3	159.5	157.3
1977	182.0	190.3	183.4	209.7	161.8	211.3	166.8	157.4	190.3	188.3	173.3	185.7
1978	197.1	203.8	196.0	226.2	173.4	227.5	182.1	171.0	207.2	206.7	192.0	207.8
1979	223.5	228.3	217.1	247.6	208.9	250.5	201.9	187.2	243.1	236.4	213.9	239.9
1980	263.7	255.9	261.8	290.1	269.5	313.2	226.3	205.4	288.7	276.9	262.7	290.0
1981	295.0	277.5	306.1	358.2	318.2	380.0	237.2	208.3	322.6	300.7	300.8	318.0

the increase in the price of food, alcoholic drink and tobacco (1974 = 100).

3 The following table gives the value of consumer expenditure in the UK from 1971 to 1981:

£ million

1971	*1972*	*1973*	*1974*	*1975*	*1976*	*1977*	*1978*	*1979*	*1980*	*1981*
59 724	63 270	66 332	65 049	64 652	64 707	64 517	68 227	71 599	71 550	71 762

Using the information calculate the index numbers of consumer expenditure for the three years 1972, 1976 and 1981 with:
(a) 1971 as the base year;
(b) 1975 as the base year.

4 Using the information in Table 7.1 (page 65) calculate an index of inland energy consumption for the three years 1980, 1981 and 1982 with 1979 as the base year.

5 Using the price indices in Exercise 3, Table 7.7 (page 79), comment on the change in prices of different methods of passenger transport from 1961 to 1981, and compare them with the changes in the Retail Price Index.

6 LAB is a labour intensive industry and CAP is a capital intensive industry. The following table gives the percentage increase in their costs from 1980 to 1984.

Cost items	*Cost distribution in 1980 percentages*		*1984% increase in costs*
	LAB	*CAP*	
Labour	70	10	50
Raw materials	20	20	80
Capital	10	70	120

You are required to calculate an index of total costs for each industry in 1984 based on 1980 = 100. Explain why you think that the results may not accurately reflect the changes which have taken place between 1980 and 1984.

10 Purpose and development of accounting

10.1 Introduction

In today's world money is the medium of exchange and the standard measure of value. It is not surprising, therefore, that all business organisations pay particular attention to their financial information; it provides the details which enable a firm to control its activities, and to assess its performance.

Accounting systems, which follow standard conventions and principles, are used by all types of organisation – nationalised industries, private companies, social clubs, etc. The essential elements of the most elementary accounting system are:

Data collection		**Data recording**		**Financial presentation**
Costs Sales Purchases	→	Double entry bookkeeping	→	Profit and loss account and balance sheet

The following three chapters outline the nature of this elementary accounting system.

10.2 Purpose of accounting – internal management

One of the main purposes in keeping accounting records is to provide information which enables the firm to be managed more effectively. Effective management is achieved by controlling the flow of resources – goods, equipment, people – through the business, and by improving the allocation of resources.

Money is flowing in and out of businesses all of the time. The constant demand which organisations have for resources means that they are constantly faced with expenses. The circular flow of money through an organisation (see Figure 10.1*) is one of the main reasons for keeping accurate and up-to-date accounting information.

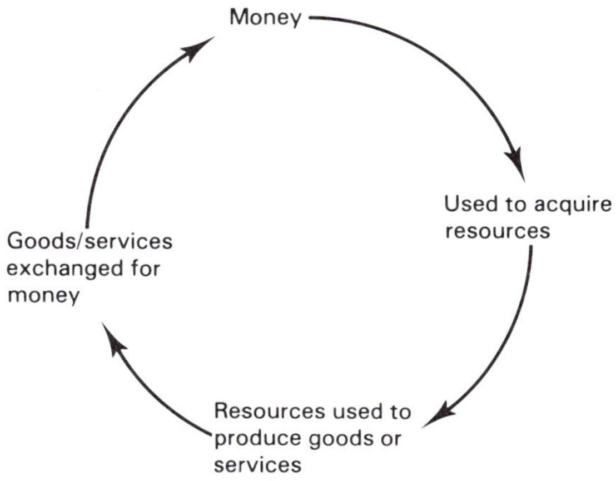

Figure 10.1 Cash flow in an organisation

By keeping a record of the flow of money through the organisation the management can assess whether the business is profitable; and, equally important, it can check whether there is sufficient revenue coming in to pay for its current productive activity.

An organisation's efficiency, or the value it gets from its use of resources, is represented by how much money the organisation spends on different items in relation to the output it gains from its expenditure. For example, if there are two breweries producing identical amounts and types of beer, the brewery with the lower costs of production would be considered to be more efficient.

A record of a firm's costs provides information which enables the management to control the firm's resources and to ensure that goods, equipment, and people are used more effectively.

10.3 Purpose of accounting – external stewardship

Most businesses are not run by the people who own them. For example, public limited companies are managed on behalf of shareholders, and nationalised industries are managed on behalf of the taxpayer. In such

* Peter Fearns, *Business Studies: An integrated approach* (Hodder and Stoughton).

cases it is essential to have some system which ensures that information is available which shows that a business is being managed properly. Accounting provides such information.

Under the Companies Acts, companies have an obligation to provide accounting information. The main obligations on a firm are to produce accounts according to accounting principles, to disclose methods of valuing assets and other information, and to present the accounts in a particular format. The overriding principle is that the accounts should give a 'true and fair view' of the state of the company.

The traditional method which is adopted to ensure that accounts do give a 'true and fair view' is to employ an external auditor who checks the books; and, if it is the case, certifies that the accounts give a 'true and fair view', and that proper books of accounts have been kept. Without accounting information the external stewardship of companies would be almost impossible.

10.4 Accounting and business activity

Accounting helps managers to keep a track of the flow of resources through a business; and, by recording the money values of all transactions, accounting has become inextricably linked to all business activity.

Figure 10.2 (similar to Figure 10.1) illustrates the circular nature of the flow of money through an organisation. Because the flow of money is recorded in a business then all transactions, in the course of business, are in effect recorded. There are, of course, for most businesses, many hundreds of transactions every week. Figure 10.2 shows purchases and sales because they are the main features of business activity; but all other types of transaction such as the payment of wages, rent, rates, taxes, insurance, transport, services to clients, etc., are also recorded.

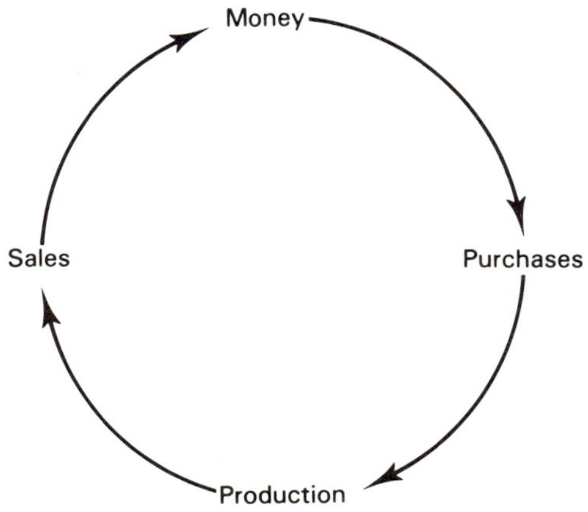

Figure 10.2 Cash flow

11 Profit and loss account and balance sheet

11.1 Introduction

'At the end of a specific period, the accounting records of all organisations are totalled and balanced; and the balances are compiled into a list which is termed a trial balance'. The trial balance does not show how profitable the firm's trading has been, but it does provide the necessary information for the compilation of the trading, profit and loss account and balance sheet.

11.2 Trading account

The *trading account* is in effect a ledger account which is used to calculate *gross* or *trading* profit or loss by deducting the cost of the goods sold from the income on sales. We shall see later in the chapter that gross profit is often an important figure in judging the efficiency of a business.

The items which are included in the trading account are:

Trading account

		£
Add	income from sales	+ sales
Deduct	costs of goods sold e.g. cost of raw materials,* wages of operatives; fuel for machines.	− direct costs
Gives	the gross profit or loss	= gross profit or loss

* In most businesses raw materials are not used up within a fixed trading period, and consequently stocks are carried from one period to the next. The cost of raw materials includes, therefore, not only the purchases made during the period but also the value of the stock held at the beginning of the period less the value of the closing stock.

The balance – gross profit or loss – on the trading account is transferred to the profit and loss account.

11.3 Profit and loss account

The purpose of the *profit and loss account* is to show the profit or loss made by a business during a given period*. Similar to the trading account, the profit and loss account is a trading account; the expenses incurred by the business are transferred from the trial balance, and shown in the profit and loss account as debit items; the gross profit and any other income are shown as credit items.

Schedule 4 of the Companies Act 1985 requires companies to present the profit and loss account in a certain format. The following shows the layout for Format 1.

	£	£
Turnover		xxx
Cost of Sales		(x)
Gross profit (or loss)		xxx
Distribution costs		(x)
Administrative expenses		(x)
Other operating income		xxx
Income from shares in group companies		xxx
Income from shares in related companies		xxx
Income from other fixed asset investments		xxx
Other interest receivable and similar income		xxx
Amounts written off investments		(x)
Interest payable and similar charges		(x)
Profit (or loss) on ordinary activities before taxation		xxx
Tax on profit or loss on ordinary activities		(x)
Profit (or loss) on ordinary activities after taxation		xxx
Extraordinary income	xxx	
Extraordinary charges	(x)	
Extraordinary profit (or loss)		xxx
Tax on extraordinary profit (or loss)		(x)
Other taxes not shown		(x)
Profit or loss for the financial year		xxx

Items shown in brackets (x) are minus figures.

* Naturally, for any business, trading is a constant activity which cannot be stopped in order that the profit can be assessed. Even so the profit and loss account is taken at a fixed point in time; consequently adjustments have to be made to expenses and to income to ensure that the account is an accurate reflection of the trading period.

For example some expenses such as wages are paid at regular intervals, and the intervals might not coincide with the final accounting period; any expenses that have accrued, and have not been paid, must be shown in the profit and loss account. Care must equally be taken to ensure that any expenses that have been paid in advance – such as insurance or rates – and are not related to the period, should not be included in the profit and loss account.

Example 11.3

The following is a trial balance as at 31 December which has been extracted from the books of M Grey, who runs a DIY shop:

	DR (£)	*CR (£)*
Cash at bank	920	
Purchases	25 129	
Sales		41 926
Rent and rates	415	
Buildings	12 000	
Debtors	4 140	
Creditors		3 291
Depreciation (van)	1 250	
Cash in hand	172	
Stock on 1 Jan	7 235	
Advertising	285	
Assistant's wages	3 400	
Light and heat	569	
Insurance	352	
Capital account		14 400
Drawings	4 000	
Bad debts provision		250
	£59 867	£59 867

Additional information

(a) The value of the closing stock is £4878.
(b) 50% of the amount paid for insurance is prepaid.
(c) The actual bad debts incurred are £120. The provision is to be adjusted to 5% of debtors.
(d) The accrued wages for the assistant are £65.

Using the information given above you are required to prepare a trading and profit and loss account for the year ended 31 December 19xx.

Answer

In order to compile the trading and profit and loss account we must select those items from the trial balance which deal with income and expenditure, and then make the necessary adjustments. At this stage we are not dealing with the assets and liabilities of the firm. See the table on the next page.

11.4 Appropriation account

Many organisations, having calculated the net profit, transfer the profit to an *appropriation account*. The purpose of this account is to show how

M Grey, Trading and profit and loss account for the year ended 31 December 19xx

	£	£
Sales		41 926
Less		
Cost of goods sold		
Purchases	25 129	
+Stock 1 Jan	7 235	
	32 364	
−Stock 31 Dec	4 878	
	27 486	27 486
Gross profit		14 440
Less		
Selling		
Depreciation	1 250	
Advertising	285	
Administration		
Rent and rates	415	
Light and heat	569	
Insurance*	176	
Wages	3 465	
Finance		
Bad debts**	71	
	6 231	6 231
Net profit		8 209

* 50% of the insurance is prepaid and, therefore, half the expenditure applies to the following year's profit and loss account.

** Calculation of bad debts:

	£
Actual	120
+New provision (5% of £4140 − 120)	201
	321
− Old provision	250
Per profit and loss account	£ 71

the net profit is to be distributed. The profits of a firm are, of course, subject to taxation. Once tax has been deducted the proprietors have the following options:

(a) Payment of dividends

A limited liability company can appropriate the profits for the payment of dividends to the shareholders.

(b) Redemption of loans and debentures

Companies often borrow money through loan or debenture stock. In such cases an annual amount is set aside out of the profits, so that on maturity a loan can be redeemed.

(c) Transfers to reserve

Many successful firms expand by 'ploughing' profits back into the business. During the course of a trading year a firm can use its profits to acquire additional resources such as buildings, equipment, vehicles or stocks of raw materials. This type of investment will be shown in the appropriation account as a transfer to reserves.

One conventional form of presentation of the appropriation account is:

Profit and loss appropriation account

Taxation		
Add	net profit	– net profit
Deduct	taxation	– taxation
Gives	the net profit after tax	= net profit after tax
Other appropriations		
Add	net profit after tax	+ net profit after tax
Add	previous balance	+ balance
Deduct	dividends proposed or paid	– dividends
Deduct	redemption of loans	– redemption
Deduct	transfers to reserve	– reserves
Gives	the balance on the profit and loss account which will be shown in the balance sheet	= balance

11.5 The balance sheet

The *balance sheet* is not an account; it is a statement of the financial position of a firm at a certain date. The balance sheet provides details of the assets, liabilities and the owners' equity. Schedule 4 of the Companies Act 1985 requires firms to disclose financial information in a specified format; and the following shows the minimum headings which are required to be included in a Balance Sheet presented in vertical Format 1:

	£	£
Called-up share capital not paid		xxx
Fixed assets		
Intangible assets	xx	
Tangible assets	xx	
Investments	xx	xxx
Current assets		
Stocks	xx	
Debtors	xx	
Investments	xx	
Cash	xx	xxx
Prepayments and accrued income		xxx
Creditors: amounts falling due within one year		(xxx)
Net current assets (liabilities)		xxx
Total assets less current liabilities		xxx
Creditors: amounts falling due after more than one year		(xxx)
Provisions for liabilities and charges		(xxx)
Accruals and deferred income		(xxx)
Net worth of the company		****
The above is financed by:		
Capital and reserves		
Called-up share capital	xx	
Share premium account	xx	
Revaluation reserve	xx	
Other reserves	xx	xxxx
Profit and loss account		xxxx
		****

Items shown in brackets (x) are minus figures.

An organisation acquires assets by incurring liabilities and by using the owners' equity; therefore the fixed and current assets equal the liabilities of a firm and its equity (which includes any reserves and retained profits). Thus if a company's books are correctly kept, then both sides of the balance sheet should balance:

$$\text{Assets} = \text{Liabilities} + \text{Equity}$$

The main aims in presenting a balance sheet are:

(a) To show how the organisation has converted money into 'real' or 'productive' assets/resources;
(b) To provide a record which allows auditors and owners to keep a check on the assets of a firm;
(c) To provide a record which can be analysed to show how the

organisation is performing. For example the balance sheet shows the proportion of loan to equity capital, as well as the balance between fixed assets and current assets, and the balance between current assets and current liabilities.
(d) To show, at a specified time, the total capital employed in the business (share capital, loans and amounts due to creditors).

Example 11.5

Using the information in example 11.3 you are required to prepare a balance sheet for M Grey as at 31 December 19xx.

Answer

Balance sheet of M Grey at 31 December 19xx

			£
Fixed assets			
Buildings			12 000
Current assets			
Stock		4 878	
Debtors	4 140		
less provision for bad debts	321		
		3 819	
Prepaid insurance		176	
Cash at bank		920	
Cash in hand		172	
			9 965
			21 965
Deduct current liabilities			
Creditors		3 291	
Accrued charges		65	
			3 356
			£18 609
Net worth of the firm			
Represented by			
Capital		14 400	
Profit for the year	8 209		
less drawings	4 000		
		4 209	£18 609

It is customary when presenting a balance sheet to show the assets and liabilities in order of liquidity (the ease with which they can be converted into cash), starting with the least liquid items.

In the examples given in this text the balance sheet is presented in a vertical format. A more traditional form of presentation is the horizontal format, which follows the double entry system: the firm's equity and liabilities are shown as debit balances and the assets are shown as credit balances. Whichever form is chosen the equation assets = liabilities + equity applies.

11.6 Manufacturing accounts

The accounts which have been dealt with so far assume that a business is concerned only with finished goods. This is not always the case. There are many firms which produce goods; and the purpose of manufacturing accounts is to show the cost of producing goods in a factory.

However, it is not always easy to identify which costs have been incurred in the manufacturing process because some costs are spread between various cost centres. For example, rent and rates apply to offices as well as to the factory. In such instances the costs have to be apportioned between the centres, and in the case of rent and rates the apportionment could be based on the amount of space used.

11.7 Manufacturing costs

The following elements of cost are generally shown in manufacturing accounts:

(a) Prime costs/direct costs
(i) Opening stock of raw materials;
(ii) Purchases of raw materials less closing stock;
(iii) Cost of raw materials carriage;
(iv) Direct wages – those incurred directly in production.

(b) Factory costs
These are prime costs plus the following indirect factory expenses:
(i) Rent and rates;
(ii) Heat, light and power;
(iii) Plant and machinery;
(iv) Depreciation;
(v) Indirect wages.

(c) Work-in-progress
Adjustment has to be made for the value of the stock which is not finished – i.e. work-in-progress.

(i) Add the value of work-in-progress at the beginning of the period;
(ii) Deduct the value of work-in-progress at the end of the period.

The value of the stocks of finished goods is shown in the trading account as explained in section 11.2.

11.8 Sources and applications of funds

Since 1971 the Accounting Standards Steering Committee have issued a series of Statements of Standard Accounting Practice (SSAP) in an attempt to standardise the preparation and publication of accounting information. SSAP 10 requires companies which have a turnover in excess of £25 000 per annum to publish a statement of the sources and application of funds.

The funds statement is necessary because to create 'a fuller understanding of a company's affairs, it is necessary also to identify the movement of assets, liabilities and capital which have taken place during the year and the resultant effect on net liquid funds.'

There are three parts to a funds statement.

(i) Sources of funds:
profit before tax;
items not involving the movement of funds
e.g. depreciation;
sales of fixed assets/investments;
funds from other sources.

(ii) Applications of funds:
dividends paid;
taxes paid;
debentures redeemed;
purchase of fixed assets/investments.

(iii) Effect on working capital:
net inflow or outflow of funds;
net liquid position.

Sources and applications of funds

	£	£
Source of funds		
Profit before tax		xx
Items not involving movement of funds		xx
Total generated from operations		xx
Funds from other sources		xx
Application of funds		
Purchase of fixed assets	(x)	
Taxation paid	(x)	
Dividends paid	(x)	
		(x)
		***
Increase/decrease in working capital		
Stock	xx	
Debtors	xx	
Creditors	(x)	
Net liquid funds	xx	
		***

Figures shown in brackets (x) are minus figures.

The funds statement provides additional analysis of the information which is already given in the profit and loss account and balance sheet. It helps to explain the changes in the strengths and weaknesses of a business by assessing the extent to which a firm's working capital (liquidity) has contracted or expanded.

The layout for the presentation of the funds statement recommended in SSAP 10 is shown on the previous page:

Example 11.8

The following information has been taken from the balance sheets for two consecutive years' trading of a medium sized manufacturing organisation.

Figures shown in £000s	Year 1	Year 2
Fixed assets		
Property	460	454
Machinery	640	680
Current assets		
Stocks	460	536
Debtors	210	300
Cash	50	92
	1820	2062
Creditors: amounts falling due within one year	290	476
Total assets less current liabilities	1530	1586
Creditors: amounts falling due after one year	540	560
Net worth of the company	990	1026
The above is financed by:		
Capital and reserves		
Called-up share capital	440	440
Profit and loss account	550	586
	990	1026

You are required to construct a statement to show the sources and uses of funds during the financial year.

Answer

Sources and applications of funds

Figures shown are in £000s

Source of funds		
Total generated from operations		36
Funds from other sources		
Long-term liability	20	
Sale of property	6	26
		62
Application of funds		
Purchase of machinery		(40)
		22
Increase/decrease in working capital		
Stock	76	
Debtors	90	
Creditors	(186)	(20)
Net liquid funds		42
		22

Figures shown in brackets (x) are minus figures.

Exercises

1 The following is a trial balance as at 31 December of a students' union shop which sells confectionery, notebooks, etc. From this information you are required to prepare a profit and loss account and balance sheet for the year.

	£Dr	£Cr
Capital account		1 400
Assistant's wages	1 079	
Purchases and sales	5 025	7 921
Debtors and creditors	824	955
Discounts received		207
Rent	480	
Sundry expenses	127	
Stock 1 January	2 592	
Bank		395
Cash in hand	86	
Equipment	355	
Repairs and maintenance	73	
Advertising	42	
Insurance	62	
Light and heat	133	
	£10 878	£10 878

Notes:
(i) $\frac{2}{3}$ of the rent is prepaid;
(ii) Stock is valued at £2692;
(iii) Accrued wages are £25.

2 The financial information which is given below has been extracted from the balance sheets of a company which produces and distributes office equipment. Using the information you are required to prepare a statement which shows the sources and applications of funds during the period covered by the balance sheets.

Figures shown in £000s	Year 1	Year 2
Fixed assets		
Property	1150	1135
Equipment	800	850
Current assets		
Stocks	575	670
Debtors	260	375
Cash	62	115
	2847	3145
Creditors: amounts falling due within one year	362	595
Total assets less current liabilities	2485	2550
Creditors: amounts falling due after one year	675	700
Net worth of the company	1810	1850
The above is financed by:		
Capital and reserves		
Called-up share capital	640	640
Profit and loss account	1170	1210
	1810	1850

3 The following trial balance is taken from Evergreens Ltd, which is a private residential home for retired people.

	£Dr	£Cr
Capital		75 000
Premises (freehold)	55 000	
Furniture	6 250	
Electricity	4 450	
Rent and rates	4 750	
Kitchen equipment	12 000	
China and cutlery	3 050	
Stock 1 Jan	1 550	
Discounts received		525
Purchases	46 150	
Purchases returns		250
Printing and stationery	1 575	
Postage and telephone	1 050	
Cash in hand	50	
Creditors		2 975
Wages and salaries	25 100	
Staff meals	3 000	
Drawings	4 250	
Receipts from residents		100 000
General sales/receipts		8 050
Miscellaneous expenses	1 750	
Professional charges	1 500	
Cash at bank	15 325	
	£186 800	£186 800

Notes:

(i) Stock at 31 December was valued at £1650

(ii) Drawings refers to the drawings of such goods as food, wines and tobacco by the proprietors, and the item should be shown as a deduction from capital on the balance sheet.

You are required to prepare a profit and loss account for the year ended 31 December 19xx, and a balance sheet as at that date.

4 The following balances are taken from Gearex plc – a manufacturing company – on 31 March, year 4.

		£
	Stock at 1 April, year 3	
	Raw materials	40 650
	Work-in-progress	19 500
	Finished goods	38 400
	Purchases/expenses for year 4	
	Raw materials	712 950
	Indirect materials	5 550
	Direct wages	159 690
	Factory power	13 650
	Factory heat and light	5 925
	Office heat and light	2 790
	Printing and stationery	3 792
	Postage and telephone	1 560
	Factory salaries	34 500
	Administration salaries	29 700
	Factory insurance	3 630
	Other insurance	1 350
	Depreciation factory machinery	15 000
	Depreciation office equipment	1 950
	Office expenses	5 040
	Selling costs	2 550
	Sales of manufactured goods	1 134 450
Additional information		
(i)	*Stock 31 March, year 4*	
	Raw materials	72 000
	Work-in-progress	23 961
	Finished goods	54 150
(ii)	*Prepayments 31 March, year 4*	
	Factory insurance	348
	Other insurance	135
(iii)	*Accrued expenses 31 March, year 4*	
	Direct wages	4 026
	Factory heat and light	591
	Office heat and light	129
	Factory power	1 050

You are required to prepare a manufacturing account, trading account, and profit and loss account for the year ended 31 March, year 4.

5 G Mead is a wine merchant and the following is the trial balance extracted from his books on 31 March 19xx:

	£Dr	£Cr
Capital account		13 400
Wages	1 832	
Stock 1 April	7 391	
Buildings	8 000	
Bank	2 531	
Cash in hand	249	
Sundry expenses	42	
Telephone	105	
Electricity	321	
Rates	744	
Delivery van	741	
Fixtures and fittings	630	
Sales		42 908
Purchases	36 214	
Discounts allowed	260	
Returns	42	180
Bad debts	26	
Insurance	123	
Creditors		6 203
Debtors	3 440	
	£62 691	£62 691

Notes:
(i) The stock on 31 March was £6591;
(ii) $\frac{1}{3}$ of the insurance is prepaid;
(iii) the accrued wages are £150;
(iv) a provision for discounts allowed is to be made at 5% of the debtors.

Using the information you are required to prepare a profit and loss account and balance sheet as at 31 March 19xx.

12 Accounting conventions

12.1 Introduction

We have seen in chapter 10 that the main purposes in accounting are to provide information which enables businesses to be managed more effectively, and to present financial statements which give a 'true and fair view' of a firm's operations. These purposes make it essential that accountants adopt concepts and conventions which are consistent, and which allow reasonable comparisons to be made within firms and between firms. The following is a summary of the accounting conventions used in modern business:

(i) *Business entity* An organisation is treated as a business unit. This unit may not conform to a legal entity, but could be a division of a very large organisation. In such instances the final accounts are published in a consolidated form.

(ii) *Accounting period* Accounting information is reported in specific periods such as monthly, quarterly, and annually.

(iii) *Going concern* It is assumed that when accounts are prepared the business will continue indefinitely. This means it is assumed that assets will continue to be used for their existing purpose.

(iv) *Historical costs* Historical costs have traditionally been used in the preparation of accounts; but changes in money values caused by inflation have made accountants reconsider this convention (see section 12.2).

(v) *Conservatism* It has been standard practice that accountants give the least favourable interpretation of any event. For example, anticipated gains are not to be recognised, but anticipated losses should be provided for. This convention can lead to an understatement of assets and profits.

(vi) *Objectivity* It is understood that accountants prepare information on actual evidence. Thus any item of expense or source of revenue must be verifiable.

(vii) *Consistency* There is, in some instances, more than one accounting method which could be adopted. For example, in section 12.5 several methods of stock valuation are listed. Where a particular accounting method has been used, then it is customary that that method should be consistently employed.

12.2 Measurement of profit and the valuation of assets

Accountants have conventionally used two definitions of profit:

(a) 'Profit or loss is the difference between total revenue from sales and the cost of the resources used.' The nature of this definition of profit is given in the examples of profit and loss accounts in section 11.3.
(b) 'Profit or loss is the increase or decrease in a firm's net assets which results from normal business activity.' The sale of existing assets and long-term capital transactions are excluded from this definition.

In spite of these definitions and the calculations given in section 11.3, it would be unrealistic to assume that the amount of profit a business makes is a straightforward calculation. Money is not constant in its value, and during inflation cash becomes an unreliable measure of value. The following is a summary of the problems caused by changes in price levels:

(i) *Value of assets* During inflation the real value of a firm's assets can increase; but, generally, increases are not recorded. Thus many asset values on balance sheets are too low.
(ii) *Depreciation* If fixed asset values are low then the depreciation charges can be too low. A major reason for setting money on one side is to provide for future purchases; inflation can make such provision inadequate. To overcome this problem many firms make current cost or replacement cost deductions from asset values.
(iii) *Stock and work in progress* The value of stock and work in progress is often no more than a subjective estimate. In a survey of published accounts made in 1981 it was discovered that six different methods of stock valuation are used in the UK.

The problems caused by inflation have been recognised as serious; and in 1970 the accountancy bodies set up an Accounting Standards Committee which publishes Statements of Standard Accounting Practice (SSAP). Nineteen SSAPs have been issued so far, and the main objectives of their publication are to improve the levels of comparability between firms by narrowing the difference between accounting methods which firms use, and to establish basic rules of accounting procedures which deal with inflation.

12.3 Valuation of stock and work in progress

As we have seen the valuation of stock is very significant in the calculation of gross profit; and constant changes in the level of prices can easily distort the accuracy of any system of stock valuation. In order to standardise the methods of stock valuation and to establish ground rules which give a fair reflection of the value of stock a Statement of Standard Accounting Practice (SSAP9) has been issued.

The basic principle is that the value of the stock should include those expenses that have been incurred in bringing the stock to its present condition and location. These costs include the purchase price, transport and handling costs, import duties and any other costs that are directly attributable less trade discounts, rebates and subsidies. Both stock and work-in-progress should be stated at cost. If, however, the net realisable value of the stock is a lower value then that value should be stated. The objective of the exercise is to ensure that the profit and loss account and the balance sheet give a fair and accurate reflection of the value of the stock and the work-in-progress.

12.4 Stock record systems

Items of stock are constantly being used and then replaced; therefore it is necessary for a business to check the amount of stock in hand at regular intervals.

Some firms, such as retailers, maintain a constant or perpetual stock record through which every transaction involving stock is analysed. The following diagram is an example of a stock record card where a constant record is maintained.

STOCK RECORD
Item: 1" Screws. Ref: 908

Date	*Purchases*			*Sales*			*Balance*		
	Units	*Unit cost*	*Total*	*Units*	*Unit cost*	*Total*	*Units*	*Unit cost*	*Total*
Bal 1/1							150	10	1500
5/1	80	10	800				230	10	2300
20/1				70	10	700	160	10	1600

Many organisations find the perpetual stock record system cumbersome and adopt a periodic check system. This involves a physical count of all of the items in stock. Each item is multiplied by its purchase price to give the value of the closing stock.

12.5 Stock valuation methods

There are a variety of methods used in business to value stock; and this section describes four methods which are used in businesses other than retailing. The popularity of the four methods varies a good deal, and the percentage shown alongside each method shows the extent to which each was used in business other than retailing in 1982 (*Survey of Published Accounts*, 1982).

FIFO (first in, first out) (45 %)

This method is based on the principle that the oldest units are the units first sold or disposed of. Thus the items in the opening balance of stock are assumed to be the first to be sold. As you can see this is a highly popular method of stock valuation. The value of the closing stock is taken to be at the later purchase prices and therefore, during rising prices, this method tends to give a relatively high stock valuation.

Average cost (16 %)

The average cost of a unit of stock is calculated by dividing the total cost of the stock in hand by the number of units. The calculation can be made within any specified accounting period.

Unit costs (6 %)

This method uses the perpetual stock record system or the periodic check system to count the actual number of items in stock. Each unit is then multiplied by its unit cost. The unit cost is the cost of purchasing or manufacturing identifiable items of stock.

LIFO (last in, first out) (3 %)

LIFO assumes that the goods which have been acquired most recently will be disposed of first. This means that the value of the closing stock is taken to be the earlier purchase price; and so, during periods of inflation, the valuation of stock tends to be relatively low.

Worked example 12.5

The following figures show a firm's stock records for the financial quarter April to June. You are required to calculate the value of the stock at the end of April using:

(a) FIFO;
(b) LIFO;
(c) Average cost.

	Purchases		Sales	
Date	Units	Unit price £	Units	Unit price £
Balance	250	10.00		
April	125	12.00	100	22.50
May	500	15.00	500	25.00
June	250	17.50	125	27.50
			725	
Balance			400	
	1125		1125	

Answer

(*a*) *FIFO*

Stock available in April		
Opening stock	250 @ £10.00 =	£2500.00
Purchases	125 @ £12.00 =	£1500.00
Total available	375	£4000.00
Stock sold in April		
Sales	100 @ £10.00 =	£1000.00
Value of remaining stock	(375 – 100 = 275 units)	
Unit costs	150 @ £10.00 =	£1500.00
	125 @ £12.00 =	£1500.00
Value (end April)	275	£3000.00

(*b*) *LIFO*

Stock available in April		
Opening stock	250 @ £10.00 =	£2500.00
Purchases	125 @ £12.00 =	£1500.00
Total available	375	£4000.00
Stock sold in April		
Sales	100 @ £12.00 =	£1200.00
Value of remaining stock	(375 – 100 = 275 units)	
Unit costs	250 @ £10.00 =	£2500.00
	25 @ £12.00 =	£ 300.00
Value (end April)	275	£2800.00

(*c*) *Average cost*

		Total cost	*Average cost*
April balance	250	£2500.00	
Purchases	125	£1500.00	
Total	375	£4000.00	£10.67
April sales	100	£1066.66	£10.67
Value of remaining stock (end April)	275 @ £10.67 =	£2933.34	

12.6 Depreciation

Depreciation is an estimate of how much an asset has been 'consumed' during an accounting period. All types of plant and machinery, motor vehicles, new technology, equipment, etc. deteriorate because they are subject to wear and tear over a period of time. In addition, an asset can be 'consumed' or depreciate because it has become obsolete or inappropriate. For example, a fairly new electric typewriter might depreciate quickly because it has become obsolete.

The extent to which an asset has deteriorated can generally only be an estimate; rarely is there a specific measure of the cost. So depreciation is a system, devised by a business, for apportioning the estimated cost of an asset over an operating period. The cost is then charged, like any other expense, against income.

Because there is a degree of judgement in assessing the charge for depreciation expense, then it is difficult to standardise how it should be calculated. SSAP12 establishes the basic rule that all assets that have a finite life should be depreciated over the accounting period during which they were used. However, the cost of the use is left to the discretion of individual organisations. Consequently there are several accounting techniques which can be used to estimate the amount of depreciation. The following section outlines two of the most common methods.

12.7 Methods of depreciation

Straight line method

This is a fixed instalment method where the cost of the asset remains constant; so a fixed amount is deducted each year. The amount which is deducted is normally a percentage of the original cost of the asset less its resale value. Thus a car costing £9000 with a resale value of £4000 after five years would be written off, over the five-year period, at a constant £1000 each year or 20% p.a.

The main advantage of this method is that it is easy to calculate and an asset can be completely written off after a specified number of years. On the other hand it is unrealistic to assume that an asset, such as a car, would deteriorate by an even amount each year.

Reducing balance method

In this method a fixed percentage is deducted from the diminishing value of the asset. Thus, using the previous example, if 20% of £5000 was deducted in the first year, then in the second year the cost of depreciation would be 20% of £4000, i.e. £800, the third year would be 20% of £3200, and so on.

This method has the advantage that it is simple to operate. In addition it ensures that the cost of the asset is high in the initial period of its life; and, of course, the asset can never be completely written off: it will always have some book value.

Example 12.7

A firm purchases a minicomputer for £40 000, and it is anticipated that the asset will not have a resale value after five years. Show the annual cost of depreciation using:

(a) The straight line method;

(b) The reducing balance method of 50%.

Answer (a)

	£
Original value	40 000
Year 1 (20% fixed cost)	8 000
Balance	32 000
Year 2 (20% fixed cost)	8 000
Balance	24 000
Year 3 (20% fixed cost)	8 000
Balance	16 000
Year 4 (20% fixed cost)	8 000
Balance	8 000
Year 5 (20% fixed cost)	8 000
Balance	—

Answer (b)

	£
Original value	40 000
Year 1 (50% cost)	20 000
Balance	20 000
Year 2 (50% cost)	10 000
Balance	10 000
Year 3 (50% cost)	5 000
Balance	5 000
Year 4 (50% cost)	2 500
Balance	2 500
Year 5 (50% cost)	1 250
Balance	1 250

12.8 Provision for bad and doubtful debts

It is inevitable in most businesses that some of the outstanding debts will not be paid. Debts that are not paid – i.e. bad debts – are treated as a loss, and are charged to the profit and loss account.

Firms learn from experience what percentage of their debts will be bad; and most businesses prudently make a provision in the accounts to cater for such losses by crediting a provision for bad debts account, and the sum allocated is deducted from 'debtors' on the balance sheet.

The purpose of the exercise, as always, is to ensure that the final accounts give a fair and realistic view of the organisation's financial position.

Worked example 12.8

At the end of a firm's financial year on 31 March, 19xx the debtors amounted to £3 000. Previous experience had shown that the firm could expect 5% of the debts would be bad. Show how you would deal with this issue in

(i) the appropriate ledger accounts;
(ii) profit and loss account; and
(iii) the balance sheet.

Answer

(i) Ledger account: provision for bad debts

31 March profit and loss account £150

(ii) Extract from the profit and loss account for the year ended 31 March 19xx

Provision for bad debts £150

(iii) Extract from the balance sheet as at 31 March 19xx

Current assets	£	
Debtors	3000	
less provision	150	£2850

Exercises

1 The following figures are taken from the stock records of a wholesale fruiterer, and they show the stock position for crates of oranges for the half-year October to March.

	Purchases		Sales	
Date	*Units crates*	*Unit price £*	*Units crates*	*Unit price £*
Balance	2000	22.00		
October	650	22.00	950	32.00
November	700	23.00	850	35.00
December	800	25.00	1300	38.50
January	400	22.00	400	30.50
February	600	24.00	350	31.50
March	550	24.00	500	31.00
			4350	
Balance			1350	
	5700		5700	

You are required to calculate the value of the stock at the end of December using:
(a) FIFO;
(b) LIFO;
(c) Average cost.

2 G Fox owns a Caravan Park and Camp Shop. The following statement shows the transactions in bottled gas which have been made at the shop during the summer period.

Statement of G Fox's trading for the half-year in gas

Purchased				*Sold*			
Date	*Units*	*Unit cost £*	*Value £*	*Date*	*Units*	*Unit cost £*	*Value £*
April	200	4.50		April	140	6.00	
May	240	4.50		May	180	6.00	
June	160	4.50		June	200	6.00	
Total	600	—		Total	520	—	
Cost of sales	520	(av)		Gross profit	520	(av)	
Stock	80						
July	280	4.60		July	200	7.00	
Aug	200	4.80		Aug	320	7.00	
Sept	120	4.40		Sept	120	6.00	
Total		—		Total		—	
Cost of sales		(av)		Gross profit		(av)	

You are required to complete the statement by inserting:

(a) the monthly purchase values;
(b) the monthly sales values;
(c) the quantity and value of the closing stock;
(d) the quantity and cost of the goods sold; and
(e) the gross profit.

Show, in the spaces provided, the average unit cost of the goods sold, and the average unit gross profit.

3 A students' union have purchased two minibuses, and the Union Council wants to know what amount to write into the annual accounts for depreciation of the two vehicles.

Using the information in the following table calculate the annual cost of depreciation for six years by:

(a) the straight line method; and
(b) the reducing balance method of 55%.

	Purchase price £	*Estimated value after six years £*
Minibus A	8500	70
Minibus B	6200	50

4 On 1 January a restaurant valued its glass and china at £7000. During the year additional glass and china were purchased for £800. The stock record at the end of the year shows that the stock of glass and china is worth £6240.

Show the glass and china account for the year, and the relevant extracts from the restaurant's profit and loss account and balance sheet.

5 At the end of a financial year on 31 March the debtors of a plant hire company amounted to £5250. On the basis of past experience it was expected that 7.5% of the debts due would prove to be bad.

Show how you would deal with the above in the appropriate ledger accounts, the profit and loss account and the balance sheet.

13 Interpretation and application of accounting information

13.1 Introduction

The apparent precision of a balance sheet is misleading. The system of accounting ensures that, providing entries are correct, the balance sheet will always balance. But the information which is disclosed can be deceptive. Fixed assets, such as premises, do not necessarily represent their actual value; similarly the value of stocks and the allowance for bad debts can only be estimated.

However, in spite of the defects which are inherent in financial records, they do provide the information with which to assess the efficiency of a firm. Several techniques are available which enable the performance of a business to be assessed; and one of the most important ones is ratio analysis.

The ratio between certain items on the profit and loss account and on the balance sheet gives a standard measure which enables a firm to compare its current efficiency either with its previous performance, or with the performance of similar organisations. There are more than 100 ratios which could be calculated, but the most useful ones are described below.

13.2 Tests of liquidity

These ratios help the organisation to analyse its cash flow.

(a) Current ratio (working capital)

current assets : current liabilities

The current ratio gives a quick method of calculating how much capital a firm has available for acquiring immediate short-term resources such as stocks of raw materials, and for the payment of work which is in progress. This ratio is known as working capital; and if it is less than 2:1 then the firm could be running into liquidity problems and might find it difficult to pay its way.

(b) Acid test ratio

current assets less stock : current liabilities

The current ratio includes stock, but stocks are not easily converted into cash. The acid test ratio excludes stock and therefore gives the relationship between highly liquid current assets and all current liabilities. Business analysts would normally look for an acid test ratio of 1:1 which signifies that the firm could immediately meet all of its current liabilities.

(c) The average period of collection of trade debts

debtors : annual sales

The ratio shows how quickly an organisation converts any money owed to it by debtors into cash in hand. For example, a ratio of 1:4 would indicate that the average period is three months, 1:2 is sixth months, and so on. The longer the period the less liquid the debts are.

13.3 Tests of profitability

Rate of return on capital

net profit : capital employed

(capital employed = fixed assets + working capital)

This ratio is the primary indicator of business performance. A company would hope to obtain a consistent return on capital which, if the organisation is successful, is higher than that achieved by similar organisations.

Profit to sales

net profit : sales or gross profit : sales

This ratio gives the relationship between profitability and sales. It would be wrong to assume that increased turnover necessarily makes a business more profitable. A profit margin obviously comes from sales, but sales arise from the productive use of resources; if goods or services are created in a costly way then increased turnover will not automatically lead to increased profitability.

Example 13.3

Using the information in the profit and loss account and balance sheet of M Grey, which are given in Examples 11.3 and 11.5, calculate the following:

(a) Current ratio;
(b) Acid test ratio;
(c) Average period of debt collection;
(d) Rate of return on capital;
(e) Gross profit to sales.

Answer

(a) £9 965 : 3 356 = 3 : 1
(b) £5 087 : 3 356 = 1.5 : 1
(c) £4 140 : 41 926 = 1 : 10 (about 5 weeks)
(d) £8 209 : 18 609 = 0.44 : 1 (or 44 %)
(e) £14 440 : 41 926 = 0.34 : 1 (or 34 %)

Although these ratios give some idea of the efficiency of the firm – for example 44 % return on capital is very good – there is an improvement in their value as indicators of performance if they can be compared either with previous accounts or with the accounts of a similar organisation.

13.4 Break-even analysis

A firm breaks even when its total costs equal total sales revenue. Once the total sales revenue exceeds total costs then the firm is making a profit. This relationship between revenue and costs is illustrated in break-even chart in Figure 13.1*.

The volume of production/sales is plotted on the horizontal axis, and the revenue and costs on the vertical axis. Figure 13.1 illustrates the amount of profit or loss at various volumes of sales/production.

There are assumptions in the construction of simple break-even charts which could be unrealistic. Figures 13.2 – 13.4 show the effect if certain assumptions are not realised.

The effects of changes in the many variables of price, costs and technology can be incorporated into break-even analysis; and a chart which does take account of these factors will be complicated but it will be more realistic and more useful.

* Figures 13.1–13.4 are taken from Peter Fearn's *Business Studies: An Integrated Approach* (Hodder and Stoughton).

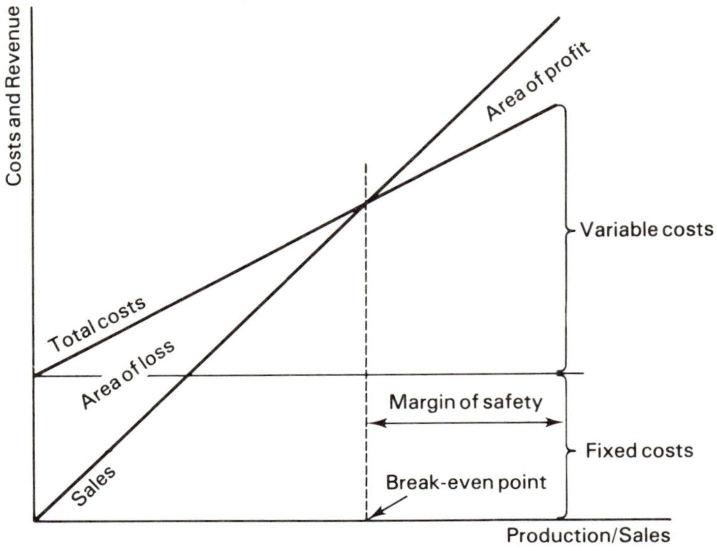

Figure 13.1 Break-even chart.

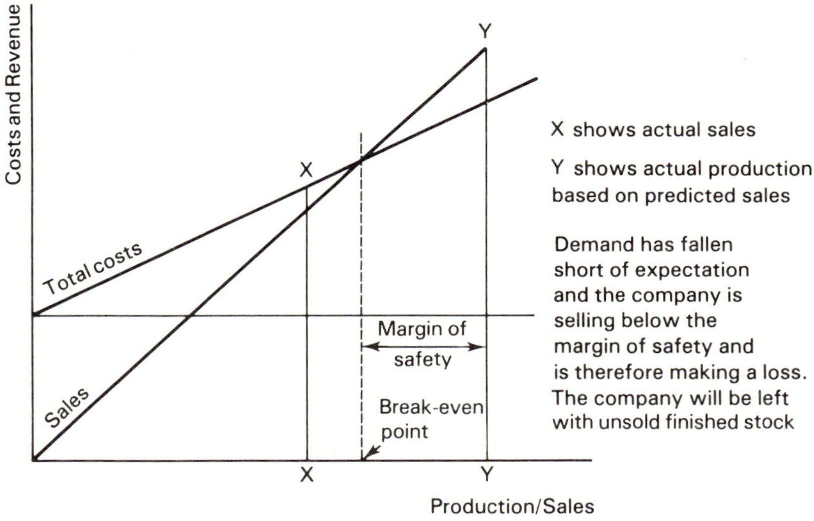

Figure 13.2 All of the goods which are produced will be sold

Worked example 13.4

The weekly production capacity of a firm is 15 000 units, and, due to a recent increase in costs, the firm's accountant has calculated that the business will break-even only if the firm is able to sell 15 000 units. The

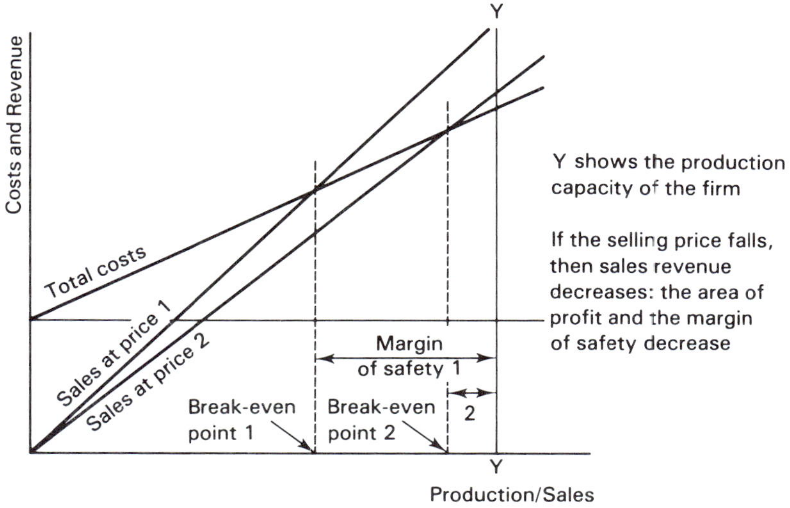

Figure 13.3 Costs, selling price and product mix remain constant

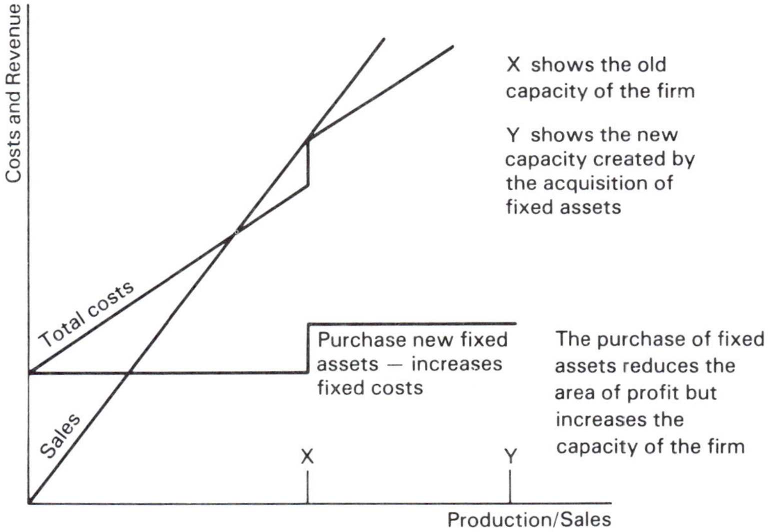

Figure 13.4 The capacity technology and the fixed assets of the organisation remain unchanged

fixed costs of the business are £75 000, and the variable costs incurred in producing each unit is £7.50. The unit selling price is £12.50.

The business has received a series of orders which exceed 15 000 units per week. The firm could increase its capacity by acquiring fixed assets valued at £14 000 from its reserves; but any production in excess of 15 000 units would add 20% to the variable cost of each extra unit which is produced. The unit selling price has to remain constant at £12.50.

You are required to construct a break-even chart which shows the output/sales required for the firm to break even if the extra orders are accepted.

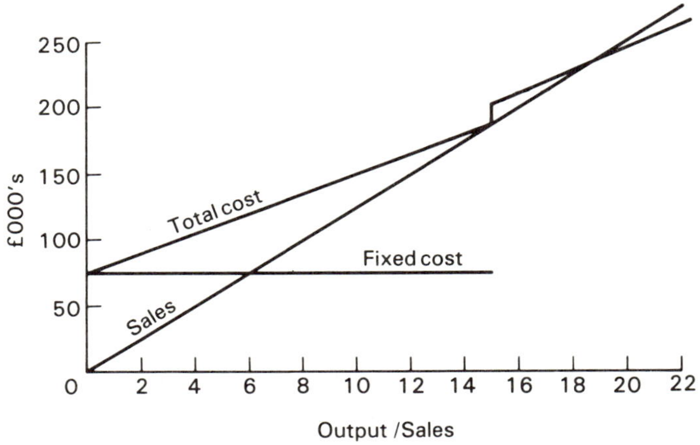

Answer 19 000 units.
Income 19 000 × £12.50 = £237 500

Costs

Fixed costs A			75 000
Fixed costs B			14 000
Variable costs	15 000	@ £7.50	112 500
Variable costs	4 000	@ £9.00	36 000
			£237 500

13.5 Budgetary control

Since finance represents the allocation of resources in an organisation, one of the best methods of improving the efficiency of a business is by controlling expenditure. Such control is frequently undertaken by applying a budgetary control system.

A budget is a plan which is based on estimates of future revenue and expenditure. It establishes the allocation of costs and expenses in relation to a given objective over a defined period of time; and it can include the employment of capital, as well as plans related to daily income and expenditure. The procedure for establishing a budget is:

(1) Define departmental or sectional goals and allocate expenditure to specific programmes. Thus a budget can relate specifically to sales, production, administration, purchasing, and marketing; or it can be a master budget.
(2) Set, in consultation with the departments, standards of operation of programmes in relation to costs.
(3) Obtain the information on actual spending in a systematic manner.
(4) Compare the actual performance (spending) with the set standard. These comparisons will take place at different times according to the nature of an organisation's operations. A manufacturing organisation will probably set annual targets and analyse them every six, or even three, months. A retail outlet might set its standards every six months, to coincide with seasonal variations in demand, and analyse them every month.
(5) Take action when marked variations occur between the actual and the planned spending, then either the plan is revised or the operation and the efficiency of the department are examined in detail. This is the stage in the budgeting process when organisations can attempt to become more efficient, by questioning the validity of departmental objectives and by considering alternative methods of operation.

The Budgetary Control Process

Define goals →	Set standards in cost terms →	Obtain information on actual costs →	Compare actual performance with plan →	Revise plans and examine other strategies
↳ Define new goals	etc.			

Example 13.5

The Bend Garage has two main areas of operation: motor vehicle service/repair and petrol/sundry sales. The following table shows the cash transactions from January to August. Using the information you are required to prepare a cash budget for the six months commencing 1 March 19xx.

Month	*Repair Sales* (£)	*Petrol Sales* (£)	*Repair Purchases* (£)	*Petrol Purchases* (£)	*Wages* (£)	*Fixed Costs* (£)
Jan	6 000	1 800	2 400	880	2 400	2 080
Feb	6 200	1 920	2 440	960	2 480	2 080
March	6 800	2 080	2 720	1 080	2 600	2 160
April	7 120	2 520	2 800	1 280	2 760	2 240
May	9 200	2 760	2 920	1 360	3 000	2 320
June	10 000	3 240	3 320	1 640	2 960	2 280
July	9 000	2 840	2 920	1 440	2 680	2 120
Aug	8 160	2 600	2 840	1 280	2 440	2 040

Additional information

(i) Assume that all the sales are cash sales.

(ii) The time lag in the payment of suppliers is 2 months. The time lag in the payment of overheads is 1 month. The time lag in the payment of wages is nil.

(iii) New garage equipment costing £2 000 is to be purchased in April and paid for the following month.

(iv) The firm's bank balance on 1 March 19xx was £6 000.

(v) In June the firm will receive annual interest on investment of £320.

Note

This is a simplified example of the nature of cash flow within a business. It is unusual for all of the sales of a firm to be cash sales: many customers, even of a garage, will be customers with accounts; and, therefore, most cash budgets are more complicated than this one.

Nevertheless, the example illustrates the importance of assessing the flow of cash, so that the company can determine whether its future cash position is going to be satisfactory. The technique of producing a cash budget makes it easier to plan for any capital expenditure and to ensure effective use of cash resources.

13.6 Investment appraisal

The survival and development of an organisation depends on the management's ability to make successful investment decisions. The collection and presentation of accurate accounting information is an essential ingredient in the investment appraisal process; and this information is supplemented by investment appraisal techniques.

The two elements that an organisation takes into account in an investment decision are the cost of the project and the expected benefits which the project is expected to bring. The cost of the project is fairly easy to estimate since the price of machinery or plant or equipment is known. Firms can also make reliable estimates of running and maintenance costs. The benefit side of a project, however, is not so easy to predict: the degree of risk, the timing of the benefits, as well as missed opportunity to invest the money elsewhere, make the assessment of the rewards from investment unreliable.

The degree of risk

Competition from other organisations makes the predictions of the rewards from an investment project unreliable. The risk of failure is high: 80% of all new products fail to become established.

The timing of the benefits

A major feature of investment decisions is the time lag between the initial investment and the eventual return. Money, in effect, buys the time between the initial outlay and the eventual return. To complicate the issue is the fact that money received at different times has a different value. The sooner an organisation receives a return, the sooner it can employ the money to earn further rewards. A delay in obtaining earnings from an investment decreases the value of the earnings. Tables have been devised which discount future money earnings back to present value, as shown in Table 13.1.

Table 13.1 A discount table showing the present value of £1.00 receivable or payable in future years

Year	*Rate of discount* (2%)	(5%)
1	0.9804	0.9524
2	0.9612	0.9070
3	0.9423	0.8638
4	0.9238	0.8227
5	0.9057	0.7835

From Table 13.1 it can be seen that the present value of £1.00 which is to be received in four years' time and discounted at 5% per annum is worth only £0.8227. Tables have been compiled for all rates of discount up to 48% and for periods up to 50 years.

13.7 Missed opportunities to invest – opportunity cost

A notion which runs through all investment decisions is the one of opportunity cost. The benefits from an investment project are produced over a number of years, and during the time the money used on the project might have been used more profitably elsewhere. The true cost of an expenditure is the lost opportunity of spending the money on alternative schemes.

Normally the benefits which would have arisen from an alternative scheme will never be known. But a common and constant indicator is the return which would have been obtained if the money had been lent to someone else, i.e. the rate of interest. If an organisation chooses to lend money rather than buy resources, it can make a reliable estimate of the reward it would obtain. When using discount tables the rates of discount vary from 1 to 48 % and a problem is which rate of discount to select. A good guide is the rate of interest one would get if the money were lent.

Table 13.1 shows quite clearly that the longer returns are delayed, the lower the present value of £1.00 becomes. This fall in value should not be confused with the falling value in money caused by inflation. Discount tables simply show how the value of the £1.00 falls at a particular rate of interest; even if the rate of inflation was zero money would still lose its value over time because delay costs either income which would have been earned had the £1.00 been 'in the hand', or the expense of interest paid on the borrowed £1.00

13.8 Pay-back

This is the crudest method of investment appraisal. The payback period is the time taken for an investment to generate sufficient revenue to recover the initial outlay. The investment programme which is selected is the one which repays the initial cost in the shortest possible time. Therefore the pay-back method emphasises the project which brings immediate reward.

Worked example 13.8

A firm has to make a decision between two investment programmes each costing £3 000. It is estimated that programme A will yield a constant, but relatively low return of £750 per annum for five years. Programme B will provide a relatively high initial return which diminishes as follows:

Year	*Programme B Return (£)*
1	1 450
2	950
3	600
4	300
5	100
Total return	3 400

Use the pay-back method of investment appraisal to decide which programme to select.

Answer
The cost of either programme is £3 000, and the one which gives the quickest return can be judged by calculating an annual cumulative return.

Year	*Programme A* Cumulative return (£)	*Programme B* Cumulative return (£)
1	750	1 450
2	1 500	2 400
3	2 250	3 000
4	3 000	3 300
5	3 750	3 400
Total return	3 750	3 400

As the table shows, the pay-back period for A is four years and for B three years. The decision is to invest in B even though after four years A provides a better return.

13.9 Average rate of return

The average rate of return is the ratio of profit (after depreciation) to capital outlay. Net profit is more commonly used than gross profit. The capital outlay can be the initial sum invested or the outflow of cash over the life of the project. Although the average rate of return is not as crude as the pay-back method, it ignores the timing of the cash flows and therefore is not ideal. Time is an important factor in all investment projects.

Worked example 13.9

A firm has to make a decision between two investment projects. The initial cost of both programmes is £2 000, and their estimated life is five years. It is predicted that the repair and maintenance costs will be constant at £200 per annum. The average annual costs and the estimated returns on each programme is:

Year	*1*	*2*	*3*	*4*	*5*	*Total*
Average capital cost	400	400	400	400	400	£2 000
Repairs and maintenance	200	200	200	200	200	£1 000
Estimated annual cost	600	600	600	600	600	£3 000
Estimated yield of A	600	600	700	1 000	1 000	£3 900
Estimated yield of B	900	800	700	600	600	£3 600

Answer
Average rate of return

	Year 1	*Year 5*
Programme A	100% (600:600)	130% (3900:3000)
Programme B	150% (900:600)	120% (3600:3000)

Using this techinique then Programme B is the preferred option even though, in the long run, Programme A provides a better average rate of return. B looks to be a safer prospect for the short term.

This method of investment appraisal is considered to be more satisfactory than the pay-back method because it pays attention to the flow of cash within a project. However the average rate of return does not take account of the incidence of the cash flows: the method becomes more effective when the timing of cash flows is taken into account.

13.10 Internal rate of return (IRR)

The pay-back method and the average rate of return method do not recognise that cash in hand is worth more than cash received in future periods. Discounted cash flow techniques (DCF) do recognise this fact, and by using discount tables cash flows can be discounted at a rate which reflects the cost of capital.

One of the most common investment appraisal techniques is the internal rate of return method, which uses discount tables to compare alternative projects. The method takes into account the cost of the project as well as the timing of the inflow of cash. IRR uses the net present value of the pound to find a rate of interest which will discount the cash flow of a proposed investment to zero.

Worked example 13.10

An investment project requires a capital outlay of £3000, and it is estimated that it will yield an annual net rate of return of £800 over a five-year period. You are required to calculate the internal rate of return.

Answer
Using discount tables we can find the net present value of the project:

Year	*Net cash flow (£)*	*Discount (@ 10%)*	*Present value (10%)*	*Discount (@ 12%)*	*Present value (12%)*
0	−3000	1.0000	−3000.0	1.0000	−3000.0
1	+ 800	0.9091	+ 727.3	0.8929	+ 714.3
2	+ 800	0.8264	+ 661.1	0.7972	+ 637.8
3	+ 800	0.7513	+ 601.0	0.7118	+ 569.4
4	+ 800	0.6830	+ 546.4	0.6355	+ 508.4
5	+ 800	0.6209	+ 496.7	0.5674	+ 453.9
Net present value of yield £			+ 32.5		− 116.2

It would appear from the above analysis that the discount rate which is likely to give a net present value to the yield of 0 is near to a rate of discount of 10%. Indeed when a rate of 10.4% is applied, as in the following table, then the IRR is 0.

Year	*Net cash flow (£)*	*Discount (@ 10.4%)*	*Present value (10.4%)*
0	−3000	1.0000	−3000.0
1	+ 800	0.9058	+ 724.6
2	+ 800	0.8205	+ 656.4
3	+ 800	0.7432	+ 594.6
4	+ 800	0.6732	+ 538.6
5	+ 800	0.6098	+ 487.8
Net present value of yield (£)			000.0*

* Figures do not add up exactly to zero because of rounding.

If the cost of the capital (plus a premium for risk since the cash flows are not guarantees but are estimates) is higher than the IRR – in this example 10.4% – then the proposed investment should be rejected.

Exercises

1 An old established manufacturing organisation Pym Engineering want their financial performance for 1970 to be analysed, and they have produced the following accounts which were produced in the traditional horizontal format.

Trading, profit and loss account for year ended 31 December 1970

				(£ *thousand*)
Stock		54	Sales	
Raw materials	510		Cash	108
Wages	150		Credit	1 440
Factory expansion	390			
		1 050		
		1 104		
Less stock		72		
Factory cost of sales		1 032		
Gross profit		516		
		1 548		1 548
Administration expenses		153	Gross profit	516
Marketing expenses		183		
Financial expenses (includes debenture int.)		15		
Net profit		165		
		516		516

Appropriation account (£ thousand)

Corporation tax	60	Net profit	165
Preference dividend (gross)	9	Balance b/fwd	21
Proposed ordinary dividend	60		
Balance c/fwd	57		
	186		186

Balance sheet at 31 December 19xx (£ thousand)

Ordinary shares @ £1.00		300	Fixed assets		510
6% Preference shares of £1.00		150			
Revenue reserves		57			
		507			
5% debentures		60	Current assets		
			Stock	72	
		567	Debtors	180	
			Cash	45	
					297
Current liabilities:					
Creditors	120				
Taxation	60				
Proposed dividend	60				
		240			
		807			807

You are required to calculate the following ratios:

(a) Return on capital employed – gross and net;
(b) Profit on sales – gross and net before tax;
(c) Working capital;
(d) Acid test ratio; and
(e) Debtors ratio.

Comment on the format of the accounts. Do you think that the presentation of the information meets the requirements of the 1985 Companies Act?

2 A petrol filling station serves up to 2 500 customers per week. The average amount spent by each customer is £10.00. The weekly costs of the business are:
(a) fixed costs (rent, rates, insurance and wages) – £4 500;
(b) variable costs (petrol) – 75% of sales.

You are required to:
(a) Construct a table which shows the amount of profit/loss per week when the garage serves 800, 1 200, 1 600, 2 000, 2 400 customers per week; and
(b) Construct a graph which shows the breakeven point.

3 At the beginning of January, Fabric plc has a bank balance of £12 000. The budgeted operating statements is as follows (£ thousand):

	Jan	*Feb*	*Mar*	*Apr*	*May*	*June*
Sales	168	192	200	216	216	240
Manufacturing expenses						
Materials	68	76	80	84	84	92
Labour	36	42	42	44	44	46
Overheads	24	30	30	32	32	34
	128	148	152	160	160	172
Increase or decrease of goods stock	(I) 4	(I) 4	(I) 4	—	—	(D) 8
	124	144	148	160	160	180
Administration	16	16	16	18	18	18
Marketing	12	12	12	14	14	14
Total expenses	152	172	176	192	192	212
Profit	16	20	24	24	24	28
Expenditure on materials						
Opening stock	8	12	16	16	20	16
Purchases	72	80	80	88	80	92
	80	92	96	104	100	108
Closing stock	12	16	16	20	16	16
	68	76	80	84	84	92

Notes: (i) Payment for purchases is made in the month following delivery.
(ii) On average, 60% of debtors pay the month after being invoiced, and 40% in the next month.
(iii) Sales for the previous November = £176 000, and for the December = £160 000.
(iv) The factory overheads include depreciation of £4 000/month.
(v) It is proposed to transfer the following sums to the capital budget – £16 000 in March, and £32 000 in June.
(vi) The payment of overheads is –

	Monthly average	*Jan*	*Apr*	*July*	*Oct*
Manufacturing	300	3 600	3 600	3 600	3 600
Administration	200	4 800	—	—	4 800

You are required to prepare a cash budget for the six-month period.

4 A farmer is considering two possible projects, each costing £21 000. His prediction of the cash inflow from both projects is:

Cash inflow	*Project A*	*Project B*
Year 1	3 000	9 000
2	4 500	7 500
3	6 000	6 000
4	9 000	4 500
5	9 000	3 000
	£31 500	£30 000

Using a rate of interest of 11% you are required to calculate the discounted cash flow for both projects; and to decide which project you would advise the farmer to invest in. Give reasons for your decision.

5 A manufacturing organisation is considering a capital project costing £220 000. The sales forecast and the relevant costs are as follows (£ thousand):

Year	*Sales*	*Cost of sales*	*Other variable costs*	*Fixed costs*	*Depreciation*
1	110	33.0	11.0	16.5	55
2	165	49.5	16.5	16.5	55
3	220	66.0	22.0	16.5	55
4	165	49.5	16.5	16.5	55
	660	198.0	66.0	66.0	220

You are required to:
(a) Assess the project by means of discounted cash flow method. Assume that the rate of interest is 12.00%;
(b) Construct a breakeven chart for the project and comment on the proposal.

14 Information technology and business operations

14.1 Information processing and change

Changes in business and the business environment constantly influenced the collection, recording and presentation of business information. These functions are subject to economic and social influences; and, above all, they are subject to changes in technology.

Technological influence

In recent years rapid progress has been made in the design and function of computer equipment (hardware) and computer programs (software). This 'second industrial revolution' is causing radical change in the way organisations operate; and one of the major changes is the way in which information is processed.

There are two significant changes. Firstly the availability of cheap, reliable microcomputers has meant that even the smallest business organisation is able to process its information electronically. The second change is that the information within a business is becoming more integrated: although the processing of accounting and statistical data is obviously a common business practice, computer programs can now combine data processing with word processing and graphical presentation. This combination is referred to as 'information processing'.

Economic influence

Developments in economics have had two major influences on business information: they have made it more necessary and they have made it more complex. As economies have developed then organisations have become increasingly more interdependent. The interdependent nature of business means that organisations can never act in isolation; the investment decisions of one organisation affect the level of activity in other organisations. Consequently, detailed information, not only about its own efficiency but also about the activities of other organisations, is vital to any business if it is to survive and prosper.

The growth of economic activity has made the nature of business information far more complex. The following list illustrates this point by showing the type of information which would be necessary to a business involved in international trade.

Example of information required in an international trade transaction
Foreign exchange rates
Insurance costs
Internal transport costs
Overseas distribution costs
Shipping or airline costs
Lists of overseas agents
Nature of government assistance, e.g. ECGD
Export and import restrictions
Home and overseas taxation
Political and economic environment of overseas customer

This list is not exhaustive, and it shows that the information required in some business transactions can be extremely complex.

Social influence

The availability of information has helped to alter society's attitudes towards the presentation and disclosure of information; it is generally felt that organisations, public and private, should disclose more details about their operations. This change in attitude has had a marked effect on the type and presentation of business and financial information.

As a result of social and political pressure the disclosure requirements of the Companies Acts and the Statements of Standard Accounting Practice (see section 12.2) have become more extensive, and the following list gives several examples of the type of financial information which firms are required to publish.

(i) *Political donations* Political and charitable contributions should be published under separate totals.
(ii) *Depreciation* The methods used to calculate depreciation, and the total charge for depreciation or the total diminution in the value of fixed assets.
(iii) *Stock* An explanation of the firm's accounting policies used to calculate the cost of stock and work in progress.
(iv) *Fixed assets* Where fixed assets are not included at historical cost, the items affected, and the basis of their valuation, should be disclosed.

The Data Protection Act 1984 is designed to regulate the use of automatically processed information which relates to people such as personal references or personnel files. Organisations are required to be open about their use of personal information.

It is not the intention of the Act that businesses should not use personal data providing they are registered and comply with certain principles. For instance, the information on people must be secure, it must be processed fairly and lawfully, and it must be adequate and relevant to its purpose. Individuals can seek compensation if a firm discloses false or unauthorised information.

14.2 The purpose of information processing

The nature and flow of information determines how 'sensitive' an organisation is to customers, employees, changes in the market, levels of sales, and so on. The purpose in processing information is to plan, record, control and report the activities of the organisation.

(i) *Planning* Managers need information to be able to plan how an organisation's resources are to be used. This can be a complex process since each department's plans must inter-relate with the other departments.
(ii) *Recording* Under the Companies Acts firms are obliged to keep financial information. In addition a business will maintain many other kinds of records dealing with such functions as sales, personnel, purchasing and production.
(iii) *Controlling* There are many activities in business where immediate or 'real time' information is necessary so that the activity can be controlled directly. These activities include stock control, budgetary control and quality control.
(iv) *Reporting* Many different kinds of reports exist in business: they range from weekly sales reports to financial reports at an Annual General Meeting. Every function within an organisation is constantly monitored and reported on. This requires firms to have accurate information produced in a fast and acceptable form.

14.3 The integrated nature of business information

The various functions within a business have to be co-ordinated, and, therefore, the information process within an organisation is an integrated one. The following table gives examples of the types of information which is processed in business, and illustrates its integrative nature.

Purpose in processing	*Type of information (examples)*
Planning	
Financial planning	Departmental costs
	Budget targets
	Income received
Production planning	Market statistics
	Orders received
	Orders dispatched
	Work in progress
Recording	
Payroll	Wages and salaries
Invoicing	Orders dispatched
	Accounts not paid
Turnover	Sales data
	Orders received
Purchases	Orders issued
Controlling	
Stock control	Purchases received
	Stocks used
	Work in progress
Budgetary control	Budget targets
	Departmental costs
Quality control	Work in progress
Reporting	
Financial reports	Sales data
	Departmental costs
	Budget targets
Personnel reports	Wages and salaries
	Training costs
	Recruitment data

14.4 The advantages of electronic data processing

For many organisations the greatest effect of technological change has been in the processing of information. During the last 30 years there has been a constant increase in the cost of administration. In the 1950s, for example, office costs amounted to 20% of total costs in most businesses; they now account for more than 50% of total costs. Organisations are looking to advances in technology to reduce these costs, and information processing is one of the main areas where technological development, especially in electronics, is having a great influence.

The reason for this influence is that electronic information processing has many advantages over traditional manual and mechanical systems of information processing. These are:

(i) *Speed* Information on almost any aspect of an organisation's activities can be recorded, sorted, analysed, stored and retrieved almost instantly.
(ii) *Accuracy* Mistakes by people are the main cause of errors in information. There is far less human involvement in electronic information processing; consequently errors are reduced. For example, standard letters to customers are typed only once and then stored for future use.
(iii) *Reliability* Microelectronic equipment is more reliable than people and mechanical equipment. People at work often make mistakes because they are tired or distracted. Mechanical equipment has many moving parts, any one of which can fail causing the machine to break down. Failure in electronic equipment is far less frequent.
(iv) *Flexibility* Electronic information processing means that the analysis of information is both accurate and sophisticated. Microprocessors can be programmed to perform many operations which previously would have been too complicated or taken too long.
(v) *Improved quality* The finished copy of written communication is greatly improved by word processing. In addition the content can be improved. For example, financial and statistical information is easily updated in reports. Information becomes less historical, and therefore more useful.

14.5 Common processes performed with business data

The processing of information within a business organisation is carried out in a set sequence. Business data has to be collected, recorded and filed. Active information, such as that dealing with stock levels or sales has to be analysed; and, at some stage, data has to be retrieved and used in communication.

The following table, by comparing traditional manual methods with electronic methods, gives examples of how developments in information technology have influenced the main functions of data processing.

Function	*Traditional methods*	*Electronic methods*
Collecting	Internal and external post Internal filing	Microcomputers or terminals collect and transmit data
Recording/sorting	Clerical/secretarial functions	Coded information can be recorded and sorted with great speed and accuracy
Analysing/calculating	Manual operation often done by managers or technicians	Computers can analyse data, such as financial ratios, budgets, etc., at high speed with great accuracy
Filing/storing	Filing by hand into card index trays or cabinets	Computers can store large volumes of data on disc or in bubbles
Retrieving	Clerical operation	Information such as stock position, bad debts, is readily available on VDU
Presenting/communicating	Secretarial operation	Electronic mail and word processing means that first-rate copies of financial reports invoices, etc. are speedily available

14.6 Collection of financial data

Since a business records every transaction, then the range of data which has to be collected can be very great. The following gives examples of the main sources of financial data:

Type of transaction	*Source of data*
Credit purchases	Invoices received
Credit sales	Invoices issued
Money due to suppliers	Orders issued/goods received note
Money due from customers/clients	Orders received/goods dispatch note
Regular expenses e.g. wages, rates, insurance	Miscellaneous items, e.g. time card, standing order
Cash and cheque transactions	Actual cash in hand, cash till details, cheque stubs, bank statements
Value of assets	Original purchase records, depreciation details, external valuation

Many companies also keep financial details of the cost of activities within sections or departments such as marketing, personnel, and production. All resources and functions should contribute to the business, and it is possible to attribute any cost to some external transactions; but in the case of internal costs such as depreciation then this can be complicated.

The reason for keeping details of costs is to provide information about the performance and efficiency of departments within the company. The method of collection varies from firm to firm, but in general internal documents as well as the sources listed above will be used in the costing process.

14.7 Flowcharting business systems

Information is the lifeblood of an organisation. It flows between suppliers and customers and within the organisation. In addition a business is part of the economic infrastructure, and it must take account of the activities of its competitors as well as general economic indicators such as the levels of unemployment, interest rates and taxation levels. In effect, every business is a system within a system.

The flow of information within a system can be charted using flowcharting symbols. These symbols are standardised and their shape represents a processing activity. The symbols in Figure 14.1 are the main ones used to indicate the sequence of operations or flow of information within a business system. In a flow diagram each symbol is linked by flowlines.

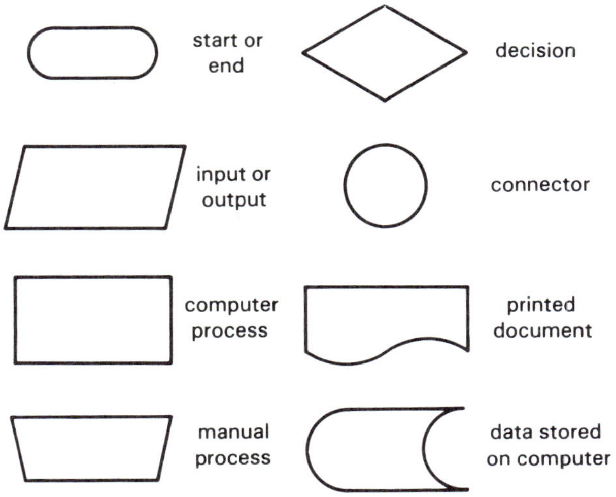

Figure 14.1 The main flow diagram symbols

Worked example

Many organisations have a product which is limited in supply and is available only at fixed periods of time. This is particularly true of those businesses engaged in travel and tourism and in entertainment. Firms such as sporting clubs, airlines, theatres and hotels control the demand from their customers by a system of reservations or booking. You are required to construct a system flow diagram which shows the flow of information in a reservation/booking system.

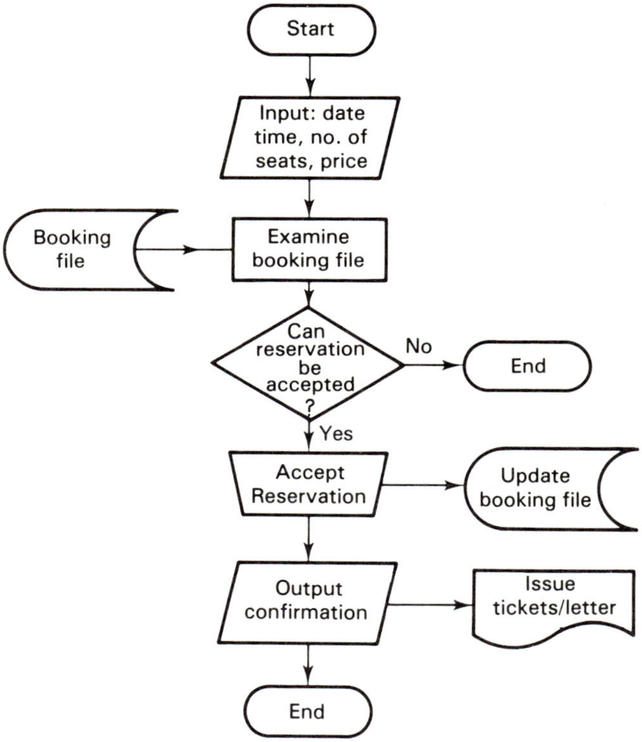

Figure 14.2 Flow diagram of a reservation/booking system

Exercises

1 Make a list of three systems with which you are familiar. The list could include issue of membership tickets of a club or society, borrowing books from the local library, ordering an item from a mail order company or withdrawing money from a savings bank. Construct a diagram which shows the flow of information within each system.

2 List the main data processing requirements of one of the following

organisations and then construct a diagram to show the integrated nature of the information:
(a) a large insurance company;
(b) a national banking organisation; and
(c) a multinational oil company.

3 Explain how information technology could/is used to process the sales/customer information of your local Electricity Board and, in your explanation, compare the modern technological process with traditional methods.

4 A medium-sized manufacturing organisation employs over 5 000 people; construct a system flow diagram to show the operations in the processing of the firm's information on wages and salaries. Please take the following notes into account:

(a) Salaried staff are automatically paid each month unless they are continuously absent for six months; they then receive half-pay.
(b) Weekly staff are able to work overtime, but they are not paid if they are absent.
(c) People engaged in sales only receive a commission on their sales.
(d) The appropriate rates of National Insurance and taxation are deducted from each employee's salary/wages.

5 Examine the effects that information systems such as Prestel could have on business operations.

15 The organisation of information processing

15.1 Types of processing system

The size and nature of business organisations vary greatly; consequently the requirements for information processing also vary greatly. There are several types of processing system, and each type is determined by the nature of the communication between the user and the computer, and whether the data is processed in large integrated blocks or in individual units.

Batch processing

The data is processed in batches rather than in single units. Business transactions are accumulated into batches, and then each batch is sorted and processed. Examples of such batches include orders received and weekly wages. This type of processing ensures rational use of manpower and equipment, but inevitably it leads to delays because an individual item of data will not be available until its batch is processed.

On-line processing

On-line systems allow the user to communicate directly with the computer; and so business transactions are recorded immediately, and the information within the system is automatically updated. Examples of this type of interactive processing are in electronic booking systems for airlines, hotels or travel agents, and in banking where the major clearing banks have an on-line system.

Interactive processing has the advantage that it avoids delays; items of information are readily available and up to date. The disadvantage is that it is more expensive to operate than batch processing systems.

Real time processing

Real time processing is where the data is processed so quickly that the results of the process can be used to control the activity. Decisions can constantly be made on the most recent information because the files are kept permanently up to date. Examples of real time processing are mainly in control systems such as railway traffic control or in the monitoring and control of production in the chemical and process industries. Real time systems require a high degree of reliability and specialised and sophisticated hardware and software; consequently they are generally very expensive.

15.2 Collection and recording of electronic data

There is a general tendency to use the terms 'information' and 'data' as though they are interchangeable. In fact 'data' provides us with a specific detail which becomes 'information' when placed in a context or structure. The integrated nature of information processing means that it is now comparatively easy to combine data and text and so provide the context to make data informative.

The first step in the electronic processing of information is the collection of details or data so that it can be converted into digital form and transferred to a computer. The conversion of data into digital form is now considerably easier than in the early days of electronic data processing when such equipment as paper tape or punched cards were the main input devices. There is now a wide variety of methods for entering information into the computer, and paper tape and punched cards are becoming obsolete.

The following are the main input methods:

Keyboard

The qwerty keyboard is probably the most common device used to enter data into computers. Almost all of the existing business microcomputer and many mainframe terminals are fitted with qwerty keyboards. The main advantage of the keyboard is that it is standardised in business and is ideal for text processing. However, the user has to have keyboard skills if the data is to be captured accurately and efficiently.

Mouse and touch screens

Keyboard skills are not easy to acquire and this disadvantage has been partly solved by the development of input devices which take advantage of the computer's processing power. The mouse and the touch screen allow the user to move the cursor around the visual display unit, and to access various parts of a computer program.

Although a keyboard is required to input data, the mouse and the touch screen minimise the need for proficiency in keyboard skills, and they have encouraged the use of microcomputers by middle and senior managers in business.

Magnetic ink character recognition (MICR)

This input method uses a highly stylised set of characters which are printed in magnetised ink; the characters are read by a special reading device. This type of data capture is very common in banking; for example, every cheque contains details on the customer's branch code, and the account and cheque number. This form of data collection is specialised, but it has the advantage of collecting specific information quickly and accurately.

Optical character recognition (OCR)

OCRs use an intensive light beam which scans letters and numbers, which are then 'recognised' by the computer. This type of input device has to overcome the problem that there are many different forms of typescript and printed material; and it will be difficult to design a system which has universal application. The most common use of OCR is in the processing of mail in the post office; but relatively cheap OCRs which can read the most common standard typeface are available for general business use.

Bar codes and magnetic strips

Bar codes are now very common on packaging in shops and supermarkets. The pattern of bars represents a number, and each type of product has its own unique code which can be read by a bar code reader which may be a laser wand or light pen. The code gives data on the size of each type of product, and the information is primarily used in stock control.

Magnetic strips are used in some shops to mark products. But they are also used by banks on cash cards or in security systems. The principles of data capture are similar to bar codes in that the data is read by a light pen and transferred automatically to a computer.

Monitoring

Real time systems require highly reliable systems of data capture since the process is controlled by the input of data. For instance, computers are used to monitor and control rail traffic, and an unreliable input could lead to disaster. Similarly monitors are used in hospitals to monitor patients in intensive care units, and failure of the input device could have severe consequences.

15.3 Storage of electronic data

An important aspect of data processing is the storage of the data, and the storage of the program of instructions for processing the data. In the early days of computers storage was a problem, but significant developments in microchip technology have meant that even small business microcomputer systems can store many millions of characters.

The following are the main methods of storing electronic data.

Magnetic tape

A magnetic tape used in data processing is similar to the audio tapes used in tape recorders; although in business operations it is wider, stronger and much longer than domestic tape. Data is stored on a magnetic tape sequentially so that access to data can be slow since the computer has to examine each record in turn; this means that this form of storage is suitable in batch processing. Up to 20 million characters can be stored on magnetic tape.

Magnetic discs

Magnetic discs, which are used in large data processing units, are generally available in a cartridge or exchangeable disc pack which consists of a number of discs. This form of storage is more expensive than magnetic tape; but, because the data can be accessed directly, it enables processing to be quick and interactive. Up to 100 million characters can be stored on magnetic discs.

Floppy discs

This is a relatively cheap form of storage, and is primarily used in small micromputer systems. The storage principles are similar to magnetic disc, although access to data is slower and storage is not as reliable as rigid magnetic disc storage. Floppy discs have the advantage that they enable large companies to decentralise some of their information processing, and are cheap enough to allow the smallest firm to have their own electronic data processing system.

Bubble stores

Bubble storage systems are still being developed. They create the possibility of storing vast amounts of data relatively cheaply. The main advantage, however, is that they allow very quick access and will help to create more interactive business/customer processes.

15.4 Types of computer

There are many different makes of computer available on the market. Some of them, especially real time microprocessors, are designed to perform a specific operation; and even generalised operations such as word processing can be performed by a dedicated or specific machine.

The main types of computer which can be used to process business information are mainframes, minicomputers and microcomputers.

Mainframe computers are large computers with an extensive facility for storing data on magnetic discs or in magnetic bubbles. Mainframes are able to perform many functions, and are the most common form of computer used in data processing in large organisations.

Minicomputers are the middle range of computers in terms of capacity and price. Consequently they are used to carry out data processing in medium-sized organisations.

Microcomputers or *personal computers* are becoming more common in business, especially in middle management and in small firms. They are cheap and technological developments have created sufficient computing power to enable managers to process departmental information in a sophisticated and integrated way.

15.5 The central processing unit

The main processing functions in an electronic data processing system are carried out by a computer's central processing unit (CPU). All computers have CPUs which have the following three main units to analyse and calculate data:

(i) The control unit executes a computer program's instructions. It examines and tests data, and co-ordinates the functions of the input and output devices.
(ii) The arithmetic unit performs any calculations which are necessary.
(iii) The main store holds the program and any data which is to be processed.

15.6 Output devices

There are a variety of peripherals which can be used to produce the output of the data processing operation. These are the main ones which are used in business:

Screens

The screen or visual display unit (VDU) is the standard output device; although, especially with the advent of portable computers, there is a wide variety of screen types. The VDU can normally display about 32 to 80 characters on a line, and up to 25 lines at any one time. The information which is presented on screens can range from teletext communications to elaborate coloured graphical displays.

Printers

Large data processing systems need very fast printing facilities to obtain hard copy, and many mainframe systems have fast printers which use laser beams or embossed belts. However, one of the most common types of printer in business is the daisy wheel printer which produces excellent letter quality output and is mainly used in word processing. Daisy wheels can be used in data processing to produce tables; but, unlike other printers, the daisy wheel is not capable of printing computer graphics.

Where a business wants to create diagrams and charts, then the computer can send its output to a dot matrix printer or ink jet printer.

Plotters

Although graphs and diagrams can be plotted on a VDU, and printed on a dot matrix printer, the results can be rough and unpolished. A graph plotter is able to produce high quality diagrams, plot complicated graphs and construct histograms and bar charts. They are often used by specialists such as seismologists or architects.

Direct output

Where a computer is used for control purposes in a real time process, direct inputs are received by monitoring devices, and the computer makes an immediate analysis and takes action through a direct output device. Examples of direct output are the raising of temperature, sounding an alarm, and operating a traffic signal or opening a valve.

15.7 Files

All forms of data processing require the system to be organised in some way. The most common way to organise information is to collect it into files. A file is therefore a collection of data relating to a specific area of business activity. As we saw in section 14.3 the list of files in any business can be long and includes data on sales, personnel, purchases and production, as well as financial data.

Each file consists of a set of records, and each record a set of fields. For example, a file of sales will contain a record for each customer and will include fields dealing with the customer's name and address, orders placed, bad debt status, etc.

15.8 Computer programs

Data processing is carried out under the control of a computer program or software. A program is held in the computer's store, and it tells the computer what operations to perform and how to perform them. There are two main types of software.

Systems software

This type of software tells the computer how to operate a particular system; and there are three categories:

(i) *Operating systems* give the computer instructions on the operation of hardware such as disc drives and printers.
(ii) *Utilities* control the file handling procedure when an applications program is being used.
(iii) *Compilers and assemblers* translate the language of the application program so that the computer can understand it.

Applications software

This type of software is dependent on a specific operating system, and when translated instructs the computer to carry out a specific application. There are a wide variety of application programs which can be purchased. In terms of data processing there are the two main types:

(i) *Spreadsheets* which enable data to be tabulated and analysed. Such programs enable the user to make elaborate and complicated calculations.
(ii) *Data base* provide firms with the facility of creating files relating to all aspects of the business.

Worked example

Imagine that you are a trainee manager in a retail unit which employs over 50 people. What fields do you think should be included in each record if the file is a data base of the firm's existing personnel?

Answer
Personnel file:
Name
Address
Age
Sex
Marital status
Present post
Grade of post
Rate of pay
Date of recruitment
Previous post
Previous employer

Exercises

1 Give examples of data processing systems which would process the information in batches, and explain the advantages and disadvantages of batch processing.

2 Explain what is meant by 'real time' processing. Your explanation should include examples taken from business.

3 List the type of files which might be used in a hospital's data processing system. Explain your choice.

4 What fields do you think should be included in the records of the following files:
(a) details of suppliers to a large company which produces electrical equipment;
(b) details of customers of a mail order company; and
(c) details of stock for stock control purposes?

5 Why do you think that applications software which integrates data processing, word processing and graphics is popular in business?

Glossary of technical terms

Accounting Standards Committee The committee was established in 1970 by the professional accountancy bodies. Its purpose is to publish approved methods of accounting, especially in relation to the problems caused by inflation (q.v.). The committee issues Statements of Standard Accounting Practice (q.v.).

Accounts overdue Those accounts to which money is owing and where the consumer/client has been reminded that the debt remains outstanding.

Accrued expenses Those expenses which have accumulated, such as wages or commission, but have not been paid. Any expenses which have accrued in an accounting period must be shown in the profit and loss account (q.v.); this is because expenses have to be accounted for in the period in which they are incurred rather than the period in which they happen to be paid.

Acid test ratio Current assets *less* stock: current liabilities. The ratio excludes stock (q.v.) from the current assets (q.v.) because the acid test is to assess whether the business can meet immediately its current liabilities (q.v.).

Appropriation account The account shows how net profit (q.v.) is to be distributed between:

Taxation;
Dividends (q.v.);
Redemption of loans (q.v.); and
Transfers to reserves (q.v.).

Assets The materials, property and rights owned by a business which have a monetary value.

Bad debts Accounts overdue (q.v.) which remain overdue for a long period and are not recovered are considered to be bad debts. Bad debts are deducted from income in the profit and loss account (q.v.); and are, therefore, treated as an expense (see provision).

Balance sheet A statement which describes the financial position of a business at a particular date (see format of accounts).

Budget A plan or forecast of income and expenditure. A budget sets targets or standards, and the actual income and expenditure is measured against these standards.

Budgetary control A management system under which differences between actual income and expenditure and the budget (q.v.) standards are investigated. The aim of the system is to control expenditure in relation to income.

Capital The amount of money invested in a business. Capital can be the proprietor's own money, or it can be borrowed via the capital market (see debentures, equity, shares).

Cash book A company's record of cash received and paid.

Cash flow The flow of purchasing power into and out of an organisation. A prudent businessman will try to estimate the inflow and outflow of cash over a given period in order to ensure that funds for purchases do not run out.

Cash transaction A business exchange in which the goods or services are paid for immediately in cash. Cash in this sense can be notes and coins or it can be cheques. Such transactions are recorded in a firm's cash book (q.v.) (see credit transaction).

Closing stock The value of the raw materials, work in progress (q.v.), and finished goods which are held in stock at the end of the accounting period (see stock, trading account).

Costs The expenses incurred in producing goods or services (see fixed cost, variable cost).

Credit transaction A business exchange in which the goods or services are not paid for immediately. Most business activity is undertaken on credit, and the transactions are recorded in a firm's day books (q.v.) and ledger account (q.v.).

Creditors The amounts due to those who have supplied goods or services to the business.

Current assets Assets (q.v.) which either exist in cash form or can be converted into cash within twelve months of the date of the balance sheet (q.v.).

Current liability An amount owed by a company which has to be paid within twelve months of the date of the balance sheet (q.v.).

Current ratio Current assets : current liabilities. The ratio is a measure of business liquidity (q.v.); and is a quick method of calculating a firm's working capital (q.v.).

Data processing The processing of information which is primarily numerical. Data processing programs are used to record, analyse and store information relating to such functions as production and marketing as well as financial information (see word processing, information processing).

Day books Lists or memorandums of credit transactions (q.v.) in sales and purchasing (see sales day book, sales returns, purchases day book, purchases returns).

Debentures Long-term loans.

Depreciation An estimate of the proportion of the value of a fixed asset (q.v.) which has been used up by such factors as wear and tear and obsolescence during the accounting period.

Direct access store A backing store where the information can be accessed quickly irrespective of the position of the data in the store. Such storage mediums as floppy discs and magnetic bubbles give the user direct or random access to data.

Discounts Deductions from the gross price of a good or service which are normally given for bulk or regular orders (see order).

Discounts allowed Discounts (q.v.) which are given by the firm to customers or clients. They are shown as an expense on the profit and loss account (q.v.).

Discounts received Discounts (q.v.) which are given by a supplier to the firm. They are shown as income on the profit and loss account (q.v.).

Dividends The amount paid to shareholders from net profit (q.v.) after taxation and other appropriations have been made (see appropriation account).

Double entry A system of bookkeeping whereby each business transaction is recorded in two accounts.

Electronic mail A communication system which is entirely dependent on the use of electronic equipment. It enables letters, reports and memorandums to be transmitted within and between organisations. The text is recorded and stored on a computer, and, on demand, the information can be transmitted to a visual display unit to be read by the recipient.

Equity The amount of capital (q.v.) invested in a business. It is shown on the balance sheet (q.v.) as the excess of assets (q.v.) over liabilities (q.v.).

Fixed asset An asset (q.v.) which a company intends to use over a long period for productive purposes; for example, land and buildings, plant and machinery.

Fixed cost A cost (q.v.) which tends to remain constant and not vary with the scale of the business operation; for example, rent.

Flowchart A diagram which represents the sequence of operations in a system or computer program.

Foreign exchange rate The price of one currency expressed in terms of another; for example, £1.00 = $1.40.

Format of accounts Smaller organisations have a choice of how to present their balance sheets: the traditional horizontal format (q.v.) or the vertical format (q.v.).

Going concern concept An assumption that a business will continue its operations for the foreseeable future.

Goodwill The value placed on the business relationships which a firm has established over a period of time. If the business is sold then goodwill is the excess which is paid over and above the value of the tangible assets.

Gross profit The surplus after the cost of the goods sold has been deducted from the total revenue obtained from sales.

Historical cost The original cost of acquiring or producing an asset (q.v.).

Horizontal format It is a requirement of the 1985 Companies Act that the format of a profit and loss account (q.v.) and balance sheet (q.v.) should either be vertical (see sections 11.3 and 11.5) or horizontal. The following is a summary of the horizontal format:

	£		£
Share capital	xxxx	Fixed assets shown at cost less depreciation	xxxx
Reserves	xxxx		
Liabilities and provisions	xxxx		
Current liabilities	xxxx	Current assets	xxxx
	£ xxxx		£ xxxx

Inflation General increases in prices and costs. Inflation causes serious problems in accounts where the convention is to record historical costs (q.v.) (see Accounting Standards Committee, Statements of Standard Accounting Practice).

Information processing A system which integrates data processing (q.v.) and word processing (q.v.). Computer application programs can be used to combine text and numerical information, and then to file, update, store and disseminate it.

Interest The cost of borrowing money.

Issued shares The value of the shares issued by a company in order to raise capital (q.v.). People or organisations who purchase shares (q.v.) (shareholders) become part owners of the company.

Invoice A document sent by a firm to customers or clients requesting payment for those goods or services it has provided in a credit transaction (q.v.). An invoice gives a business useful information such as the customer's order number, date of purchase, details of the goods supplied, any discounts (q.v.), as well as the price of the goods or service.

Journal A record of any business transaction which cannot be recorded in the other accounting books.

Ledger accounts A record of the main trading transactions. The ledger accounts are divided into three types:

Real accounts (q.v.);
Personal accounts (q.v.); and
Nominal accounts (q.v.).

Liability An amount which is owed.

Limited liability A limitation on an investor's risk. Limited liability limits the extent of an investor's risk to the amount of capital (q.v.) which the investor puts into a business.

Liquidation The legal process by which a business is dissolved. The assets (q.v.) of the business are converted into cash, i.e. liquidated.

Liquidity The ease with which an asset (q.v.) can be converted into cash. Current assets (q.v.) are highly liquid; fixed assets (q.v.) have a low liquidity.

Microprocessor An integrated circuit which contains the control unit, the arithmetic logic unit and possibly the memory of a computer.

Net profit The surplus left after expenses and costs have been deducted from all sources of income. Net profit can be shown before taxation has been deducted (pre-tax profit), or after the deduction of taxation (post-tax profit).

Nominal accounts A record in the ledger (q.v.) of gains or loans made, and of expenses incurred by a business.

Opening stock The value of raw materials, work in progress and finished goods held in stock at the beginning of an accounting period (see stock, trading account, work in progress, section 11.2).

Order Request by a customer or client for goods or services (see orders received, orders issued).

Orders issued Those orders sent by the business to suppliers (purchases) requesting them to provide goods or services.

Orders received Those orders to supply goods or services (sales) which a business has received from customers or clients.

Overhead A cost which cannot be attributed directly to any part of a firm's operations.

Personal accounts Records in the ledger (q.v.) of the credit transactions (q.v.) between suppliers, customers and clients; and they include those accounts which record sales and purchases.

Prepayment Part of an expense which is payment for goods or services which are to be supplied during the following trading period. For example, many quarterly or half-yearly bills such as rent and rates fall into this category. A prepayment is carried forward as a current asset (q.v.) in the balance sheet (q.v.), and is recognised as an expense in the accounting period in which the benefit will be derived from it.

Prestel The tradename of British Telecom's Viewdata system (q.v.). It is a computer based information access system. With Prestel, people can communicate and engage in business transactions: sellers can display details of goods and services and buyers can, in some instances, place direct orders.

Profit and loss account A statement which is a summary of the income earned by a business, and the costs and expenses incurred in earning it during an accounting period.

Profit to sales ratio This ratio can either be net profit:sales, or gross profit:sales. It shows the relationship between profitability and sales.

Provision The amount a business is prepared to deduct as an expense on the profit and loss account (q.v.) in respect of any known or estimated loss or liability (q.v.); e.g. bad debts (q.v.).

Purchase day book A daily list of those transactions where a firm has acquired goods or services on credit. The list is not part of the double entry system: this system is implemented by posting the details to the purchases account and to the appropriate personal accounts (q.v.) (see day books, credit transactions).

Purchases returns The goods a business returns to a supplier. This is done for several reasons, but primarily it is because the goods are defective or not as ordered. Thus usual practice is for a business to receive a credit note from the supplier to the value of the goods returned. The total value of the credit notes is, of course, a credit balance.

Rate of return The ratio net profit : capital employed. The capital employed is fixed assets (q.v.) plus working capital (q.v.).

Ratios The ratio between items on the profit and loss account (q.v.) and the balance sheet (q.v.) gives a standard measure of business performance (see current ratio, acid test ratio, profit to sales ratio).

Real accounts A record in the ledger accounts (q.v.) of the transactions which deal with real or tangible assets such as plant and machinery.

Real-time processing A system where the information is processed immediately to give almost instantaneous output. Real-time processing is used to control such operations as chemical production, traffic control and reservation systems.

Redemption of loans Final payment on a loan or debenture (q.v.).

Reserves The accumulated profit which has been retained by the business for general or specific purposes (see appropriation account).

Sales day book A daily list of those transactions where a firm has sold goods or services on credit. The list is not part of the double entry system; this system is implemented by posting the details to the sales account and to the appropriate personal accounts (q.v.) (see day books, credit transactions).

Sales returns The goods returned to a business by customers. This is done for several reasons, but primarily it is because the goods are defective or not as ordered. The usual practice is for the business to issue a credit note to the customer to the value of the goods returned. The total value of the credit notes issued for sales returns is a debit balance.

Serial access store A storage medium where the time taken to access an item of information depends on its position in the backing store. It is slower but usually cheaper than direct access storage (q.v.). The most common form of serial access storage is magnetic tape.

Shares Equal parts into which the capital (q.v.) of a company is divided. The holder of a share is then entitled to a proportion of the profits.

Software A set of instructions which tells a computer how to perform a certain task. Business application programs such as spreadsheets and data bases are software.

Statements of Standard Accounting Practice (SSAP) These are issued by the Accounting Standards Committee (q.v.) and describe the methods of accounting which are approved by the accountancy bodies.

Stock It is defined by Statements of Standard Accounting Practice (q.v.) as:

(a) goods or other assets (q.v.) purchased for resale;
(b) consumable stores;
(c) raw materials and components purchased for incorporation into products for sale;
(d) products and services in intermediate stages of completion;
(e) finished goods.

(see work in progress, section 11.2).

Teletext The information in a teletext system is transmitted in the same way as normal television signals. Teletext receivers pick up the information and display it on a TV screen. Unlike Viewdata (q.v.) the communication is only one way, i.e. by the transmittor.

Terminal An input/output device which provides a direct link between a computer and the user. Terminals can be located at great distances from the computer, and this is known as remote access.

Trade discounts (see discounts).

Trading account A ledger account (q.v.) which is used to calculate gross profit (q.v.) or loss by deducting the cost of the goods sold from the income on sales.

Turnover Revenue from sales.

Variable cost A cost that changes in response to changes in business activity; for example, purchase of raw materials.

Vertical format It is a requirement of the 1985 Companies Act that the format of the profit and loss account (q.v.) and balance sheet (q.v.) should be either vertical or horizontal (q.v.) (see sections 11.3 and 11.5).

Viewdata A system of electronic communication. The information is stored in a central computer and is transmitted by telephone. The information is displayed on a TV monitor or visual display unit which has been adapted to receive the electronic signals. (see Prestel, Teletext.)

Word processing The electronic processing of text. A word processing program allows the user to store, edit and manipulate business documents such as letters, reports and memorandums. (see data processing, information processing.)

Working capital Current assets less current liabilities. The amount of working capital is constantly changing in response to changes in the day-to-day business of a firm. It has a crucial role because it represents the amount a business needs to generate in order to pay for its stock (q.v.), debtors and work in progress (q.v.).

Work in progress Goods or services which are still being produced at the date of the balance sheet (q.v.). Although work in progress is often cited as an independent asset, it is recognised as part of a firm's stock (q.v.).

Twenty assignments

Introduction

This section includes 20 cross-modular assignments. The format of each is very similar. The purpose of a standard format is to ensure that B/TEC's requirements in the structure of assignments is met. Thus each assignment has the following elements:

Post

There has been an attempt in each assignment to encourage the student to assume a position within an organisation which is realistic; and therefore most of the posts are of a kind which students would probably encounter early in their careers.

Organisation

Each assignment is set within an organisational context. The 20 assignments include a wide range of settings such as small businesses, local authorities, and large multinational organisations. This wide range should enable the student to understand that business studies apply to a very diverse range of organisational activity.

Problem

Many problems in business which require the application of numeracy and accounting techniques are solved in a sophisticated and technical manner; and it could be argued that problems set at a basic or elementary level are artificial. To some extent this point of view is a fair view of the problems set in these assignments; the level of the post and the nature of the specific objectives which are being tested can restrict reality. Nevertheless, the following 20 assignments pose problems which enable the student to apply numerical and accounting skills and understanding to business problems.

Recipient

All of the assignments require communication skills to be used; and the 'recipient' in this context helps the student to identify the people who will read his/her finished work, and then to construct his/her response accordingly.

Tasks

Included in each assignment is a set of tasks and additional material such as tables and charts. The tasks and the supporting material provide a framework for assessing a student's understanding of specific aspects of business numeracy and finance.

It must be stressed, however, that the tasks and the material which are given provide a framework. For instance, it is not intended that they should be the only tasks to be covered or that all of the tasks listed are equally necessary. Secondly, quite a few of the tasks deliberately require the student or the teacher to make further assumptions and to conduct additional research. The reason for this open-ended flexibility is to encourage teachers to adapt the assignment to their own scheme of work and their students' needs. The assignments present the teacher with ideas for developing and assessing the learning of business studies; and it is hoped that they will be accepted and used in this spirit.

List of assignments

1 A simple budget
2 Trends in employment
3 Hire or purchase
4 Exports and capital formation
5 Advertising expenditure
6 The cost of advertising
7 Local rates
8 Road accidents
9 Television advertising
10 Break-even charts
11 Health care
12 Visit to London
13 Consumers' expenditure
14 Accounting information and the microcomputer
15 The flow of financial information
16 Cash flow
17 Comparison of performance
18 The sports and social club
19 Seaside restaurant
20 Ratio analysis

Assignment 1

A simple budget

Post

Assume that you are employed in an estate agent's office as a general assistant, and you are studying to gain a professional qualification.

Organisation

The organisation is a small estate agency which employs two partners, three general assistants and two clerical assistants/secretaries.

Problem

The partners want to introduce a simple system of budgetary control. They know that accountancy is included in your studies, and they have given you the details which are attached and asked you to write a report along the lines given below.

Recipients

The two partners obviously know a good deal about the business, but their knowledge of accounts is weak; therefore your report should be written for a reader who has little knowledge of budgetary control.

Tasks

Using the information in the tables below:

(1) Prepare a simple budget for a 12-month period.
(2) Calculate each item of expenditure as a proportion of total annual expenditure.
(3) Compile a report which explains the purpose of accounting as an information system for internal management; and it should also explain how the simple budgetary control system should be operated.

The following tables give the actual revenue and the typical expenditure over the past 12 months. Your budget programme should show target figures for each month, and these targets should take account of the anticipated changes which are also listed.

Revenue

Month	*(£)*	*Expected increase (%)*
1	10 256	3.5
2	12 894	3.5
3	13 562	3·5
4	14 556	3.5
5	15 660	3.5
6	15 003	3.5
7	14 012	3.5
8	10 669	3.5
9	11 293	3.5
10	12 401	3.5
11	13 753	3.5
12	9 872	3.5

Expenditure (typical month)

	(£)	*(%)*
Salaries	4820	4.0
Wages	700	4.0
Advertising	1500	5.5
Telephone	400	6.0
Petrol	500	7.5
Depreciation	2100	0.0
Printing and stationery	800	2.5
Miscellaneous	500	5.0

Other payments

	(£)	*(%)*
Rent–half-yearly (1, 7)	525	0.0
Rates–half-yearly (4, 10)	623	8.0
Electricity–quarterly (3, 6, 9, 12)	140	6.0
Insurance–annually (1)	250	0.0

Assignment 2

Trends in employment

Post

Assume that you have recently been employed as a clerical assistant in the local authority's careers guidance office.

Organisation

The careers guidance office is part of the local government's education service. Most of its clients are aged 16–19, and it works very closely with the local schools and colleges as well as with industry and commerce.

Problem

Your immediate superior is secretary to the local Schools and Industry Liaison Committee, and in that capacity he has been asked to prepare a series of lectures on the theme of 'trends in employment'. He has found that he is short of time to prepare the material and has asked you to help. His specific requests are given below.

Recipient

The material is to be specifically produced for your immediate superior, and therefore you must be prepared to have it altered or amended.

Tasks

The tasks require that you use the table on page 177.

(1) Using the table calculate the percentages of 'employees in employment' for all categories for 1961, 1971 and 1981.
(2) Using your results from Task 1 construct an appropriate diagram which illustrates the changes in employment which have taken place during the 20-year period.
(3) Carry out research to find any other diagrams or published data which would help to depict 'trends in employment'. You should write a brief interpretation of any diagrams or tables you find.

Employees in employment: by industry[a]

United Kingdom (thousands)

	1961	*1971*	*1976*	*1980*	*1981*	*1982*[b]		
						Males	*Females*	*All*
Agriculture, forestry, and fishing	710	432	393	360	351	265	88	354
Mining and quarrying	727	396	348	349	338	308	18	326
Manufacturing								
Food, drink, and tobacco	793	770	714	690	646	374	249	622
Chemicals, coal, and petroleum products	499	482	461	472	435	302	113	415
Metal manufacture	643	557	469	399	323	262	33	295
Engineering and allied industries	3 654	3 615	3 269	3 171	2 814	2 094	552	2 646
Textiles, leather, and clothing	1 444	1 124	935	777	653	248	368	616
Rest of manufacturing	1 508	1 511	1 399	1 332	1 217	828	330	1 158
Total manufacturing	8 540	8 058	7 246	6 840	6 087	4 107	1 645	5 752
Construction	1 485	1 262	1 309	1 278	1 143	934	116	1 049
Gas, electricity, and water	389	377	353	351	347	272	68	340
Services								
Transport and communication	1 678	1 568	1 475	1 505	1 443	1 111	272	1 383
Distributive trades	2 767	2 610	2 723	2 877	2 767	1 206	1 500	2 706
Insurance, banking, and finance	684	976	1 103	1 313	1 316	629	692	1 321
Professional and scientific services	2 124	2 989	3 655	3 766	3 757	1 169	2 599	3 768
Miscellaneous services	1 819	1 946	2 299	2 629	2 579	1 036	1 518	2 554
Public administration	1 311	1 509	1 631	1 592	1 573	952	598	1 549
Total services	10 382	11 597	12 886	13 681	13 435	6 103	7 179	13 282
All industries and services	22 233	22 122	22 543[c]	22 859	21 701	11 989	9 115	21 103

[a] As at June each year.

[b] 1982 estimates are provisional. The basic series given above may underestimate the level of employment (mainly in service industries). Supplementary series, which include an allowance for undercounting, show 21 223 employees, of which 5 764 were in manufacturing and 13 390 in services. See article in June 1983 edition of the *Employment Gazette*.

[c] includes 8 700 employees who were not allocated to individual industry groups.

Source: Department of Employment; Department of Manpower Services (Northern Ireland).

Assignment 3

Hire or purchase

Post

You are employed as a part-time volunteer in a local community centre.

Organisation

The centre mainly caters for the old, the infirm and the disabled in the local community. It organises activities such as whist drives, bingo, old-time dancing and shopping expeditions. Although it is partly funded by the local authority, the organising committee stages events to raise finance.

Problem

The centre has hired a minibus for various purposes; and the organisers now feel that it is probably worthwhile to purchase a bus rather than hire one. You have been asked to sort out the information and to present your recommendations.

Recipients

Your recommendations will be made to the organising committee which consists of representatives from the local council, welfare officers, and volunteers.

Tasks

(1) Using the information below calculate the cost of the alternatives over a four-year period.
(2) Construct a graph which compares the total cost of each alternative over four years. Present a report and diagram in a format which is easy to understand. Your report should compare the advantages and disadvantages of each option.

Hire or purchase a 15-seater minibus

Type of minibus	*Cost per annum (£)*			
	year 1	*year 2*	*year 3*	*year 4*
Hire				
Daily rate (150 days)	3 000	3 300	3 630	3 993
Mileage charge	1 000	1 100	1 210	1 331
Insurance	400	440	484	533
New minibus				
Capital value	8 000	6 000	4 800	4 080
Depreciation	25%	20%	15%	10%
Routine servicing	5%	5%	5%	10%
Maintenance/spares	—	5%	10%	15%
Insurance	1%	1%	1%	1%
Interest charges	10%	10%	10%	10%
Second-hand low mileage				
Capital value	5 000	4 250	3 825	3 443
Depreciation	15%	10%	10%	10%
Routine servicing	5%	10%	15%	15%
Maintenance/spares	15%	15%	20%	25%
Insurance	1%	1%	1%	1%
Interest charges	10%	10%	10%	10%
Second-hand high mileage				
Capital values	4 000	3 600	3 240	2 916
Depreciation	10%	10%	10%	10%
Routine servicing	20%	20%	25%	25%
Maintenance/spares	20%	25%	30%	30%
Insurance	1%	1%	1%	1%
Interest charges	10%	10%	10%	10%

Currently the minibus is hired three days each week, and the average annual mileage is 6 000 miles. It is anticipated that minibus hire charges will increase by 10.0% per annum, this increase is shown in the table. Other costs are shown as percentages of the existing value of the minibus. Any assessment of the total annual cost should exclude the capital value.

Assignment 4

Exports and capital formation

Post

Assume that you are an active student member of a professional body.

Organisation

The student members meet regularly on a social basis, and they also arrange discussion groups, lectures, and conferences. Most of the topics which are discussed relate to the requirements of the professional body's examinations.

Problem

The secretary has asked you to lead a discussion at the next meeting of the students. The topic is 'the exporting performance of Britain since 1965'.

Recipients

The knowledge of business studies of the people taking part in the discussion is similar to yours. It is not expected that the discussion will be very technical, nevertheless a background knowledge of economics and other aspects of business will be expected.

Tasks

The secretary of the students' members has found some old statistics which give the UK's exports and capital formation from 1965 to 1975; and he has asked you to structure your contribution along the following lines.

(1) Using published material obtain the equivalent statistics for exports and capital formation from 1975 onwards and then plot a scatter diagram of the current prices of the two variables. Assess whether there is a relationship between the two, and which, if any, is the dependent variable.
(2) Express the exports at 1970 prices, and briefly describe to the group the advantages of expressing the figures in such a way.
(3) Using your diagram and statistics as an aid give an oral presentation of your analysis to your fellow students, and encourage them to discuss the issues.

United Kingdom gross domestic fixed capital formation, 1965–75

	Current prices (£m)	*1970 prices (£m)*
1965	6 504	7 900
1966	6 922	8 097
1967	7 523	8 780
1968	8 200	9 182
1969	8 590	9 216
1970	9 453	9 453
1971	10 515	9 681
1972	11 680	9 870
1973	14 148	10 279
1974	16 633	10 087
1975	20 510	9 967

Visible exports of the United Kingdom, 1965–75

	Current prices (£m)
1965	4 848
1966	5 203
1967	5 139
1968	6 282
1969	7 075
1970	7 907
1971	8 810
1972	9 141
1973	11 772
1974	15 899
1975	18 768

Assignment 5
Advertising expenditure

Post

Assume that you are employed as a management trainee in a multinational company, and that as part of your training and development you have been seconded to the marketing division.

Organisation

The company produces a diverse range of products which are marketed through subsidiary organisations on a world-wide basis. The marketing division is the most prestigious division in the organisation, and it takes pride in contributing articles to the organisation's 'in-house' journal which is published every quarter.

Problem

An article in the previous quarter's issue of the journal criticised, in an indirect way, the dominance of the marketing function within the organisation and directly questioned the value of the company's expenditure on advertising.

Although the marketing division's director does not want to become involved in an interdepartmental debate he would like the journal to have a contribution which presents a generalised case for advertising expenditure, and you have been requested to write the article. In order to help you with the article you have been given the following table which shows the results of a survey of advertising expenditure in the UK in 1982.

Recipients

The journal is circulated throughout the organisation, and is mainly read by the clerical and managerial staff.

Tasks

You are required to:

(1) Explain the main determinants of the composition of a market.
(2) Using semi-logarithmic graph paper construct a chart which compares the total expenditure on advertising from 1952 to 1982 with both the Gross National Product and total consumer expenditure for the same period. You can use either current prices or 1975 prices, but you must explain the reasons for your choice.
(3) Using your chart, and any other relevant information, formulate a rational argument which justifies expenditure on advertising.

You will see that the table gives both consumer expenditure and Gross National Product as a percentage of expenditure on advertising. In order to obtain the total consumer expenditure and GNP you must either convert the percentages or use a standard reference of published government statistics such as the *Annual Abstract*.

Total advertising expenditure in the UK and its relation to consumer expenditure and Gross National Product, 1952–82

Year	*Total (£m) expenditure 1975 prices**	*Advertising (TAE): current*	*TAE as % of consumer expenditure*	*TAE as % of GNP*
1952	N/A	123	1.15	0.89
1956	N/A	197	1.43	1.08
1960	N/A	323	1.91	1.43
1961	897	338	1.90	1.40
1962	885	348	1.84	1.38
1963	925	371	1.84	1.38
1964	1005	416	1.94	1.42
1965	1002	435	1.90	1.39
1966	991	447	1.84	1.35
1967	976	451	1.77	1.29
1968	1039	503	1.83	1.34
1969	1067	544	1.86	1.37
1970	1022	554	1.74	1.27
1971	997	591	1.66	1.20
1972	1113	708	1.76	1.28
1973	1259	874	1.91	1.36
1974	1118	900	1.72	1.21
1975	967	967	1.50	1.03
1976	1020	1188	1.59	1.07
1977	1110	1499	1.75	1.19
1978	1254	1834	1.86	1.27
1979	1285	2131	1.82	1.27
1980	1306	2555	1.89	1.32
1981	1287	2818	1.88	1.34
1982	1316	3126	N/A	N/A

* Figures in this column are obtained by deflating the current price figures by the retail price index.

Assignment 6

The cost of advertising

Post

Assume that you are a member of the office staff in the sales office of a medium-sized organisation.

Organisation

The organisation is a privately owned company which runs over 40 garden centres. These centres are located mainly in the Midlands; but the firm intends to become established on a national basis. Up to the present time the firm's main advertising has been in the local press.

Problem

The company has decided to open a new large garden centre in your area. It is intended that the opening will be a grand affair with the purpose of creating as much publicity for the organisation as possible. One of the problems is to decide which forms of advertising to use.

Recipient

The managing director has recently read an advertising journal which included a table of 'advertising expenditure in the UK, 1978–82'. He found the explanation, given with the table, fairly technical; and he has asked you to complete the tasks, which are given below, and to let him have the results.

Tasks

You are required to write a report which includes:

(1) a simplified explanation of the table. Your explanation should include a summary of how the information is compiled, as well as an example of what is meant by 'index' and 'weighted';
(2) details, in tabular form, of the costs of the following forms of advertising:

national press;
local press;
local 'free' newspapers; and
Post Office mail.

Advertising Association TV Rates, 1978–82

Year	*Quarter*	*CHM (million)*	*Net Cost (£ 000)*	*Cost per 000 CHM (£)*
1978	1	36 884	83 181	2.255
	2	30 101	85 623	2.845
	3	27 880	81 782	2.933
	4	34 376	112 419	3.270
Total		129 241	363 005	2.809
1979	1	37 414	90 223	2.411
	2	31 445	106 497	3.387
	3	10 739	34 122	3.177
	4	23 810	115 954	4.870
Total		103 408	346 796	3.354
1980	1	35 355	135 199	3.824
	2	29 984	137 501	4.586
	3	24 912	101 227	4.063
	4	32 461	155 384	4.787
		122 712	529 311	4.313
Total				
1981	1	35 157	130 229	3.706
	2	29 906	149 425	4.996
	3	27 387	126 841	4.631
	4	32 275	204 657	6.341
Total		124 725	611 222	4.900
1982	1	34 605	163 746	4.732
	2	32 158	162 535	5.054
	3	25 196	148 942	5.911
	4	32 280	221 946	6.876
Total		124 239	697 169	5.612

* *Source*: International Journal of Advertising, June 1983
The Index of Television rates is based on data for the number of commercial minutes transmitted in the year, weighted by the number of homes tuned to each minute. These commercial home minute (CHM) data are then divided into the annual net revenue data to produce a figure of actual cost per commercial minute per thousand homes.

Your table should include an estimate of the potential number of customers who would see the advertising;
(3) a recommendation of which form, if any, of advertising to use. Your recommendation should be substantiated by an explanation of the principal factors that influence the demand for garden centres.

Assignment 7

Local rates

Post

Assume that you are the secretary of a local ratepayers' reform group.

Organisation

The Ratepayers' Reform Group is an association which has recently formed. The main aim of the Group is to act as a pressure group to bring about a reform of the rating system. Two additional aims of the Group are firstly to educate the local population about the British system of rates, and to ensure that information is available about local council spending decisions to enable people to put these into the national context.

Problem

The most pressing problem which faces the group is that it has very few members. In order to increase membership you have decided to design a leaflet which will inform ratepayers of the Group's aims; and it will explain the structure of the rating system in the UK, and will put your local authority's provision into the national context.

Recipients

The Group intends to deliver the leaflet to every household in the local community. They hope to recruit young people aged 16–19 as well as adults.

Tasks

It has been decided that the following should be included in the leaflet.

(1) A brief, but persuasive, explanation of the aims of the organisation.

Your explanation should include a list of the forms of pressure the Group will use.
(2) A comparison of the local expenditure and income with similar details from two other local authorities. These details are contained within the table below. This requires a diagram to be constructed from the raw data which shows the similarities and the differences in income and expenditure, and a concise explanation of why such differences occur.
(3) A comparison, using diagrams, of the local income and expenditure pattern with the national pattern.

Income and expenditure of South Yorkshire County Council and Somerset County Council, 1983/84

	South Yorks (£267 m)	*Somerset (£151m)*
Income (%)		
Government grants (%)	47	50
Local rates (%)	39	37
Fares, charges and other income (%)	14	13
Expenditure (£m)		
Education (£m)	—	92.2
Social services (£m)	—	16.0
Planning and Transport (£m)	97.3	14.1
Police (£m)	59.5	7.8
Fire (£m)	16.1	3.7
Highways (£m)	63.0	—
Other services (£m)	31.1	17.2
Total	267.0	151.0
Manpower (actual)		
Education	—	6 937
Social services	—	1 639
Transport	5 400	—
Police	4 388	—
Fire	1 492	259
Highways	—	835
Others	3 911	1 081
Total	15 191	10 751

Assignment 8

Road accidents

Post

Assume that you are a member of an accident prevention group.

Organisation

The aim of the Accident Prevention Group is to inform young people of the dangers of accidents at work, in the home and on the road. It has a nationwide membership which is steadily increasing.

Problem

The central committee of the group is mounting a national campaign which is designed to inform motor cyclists of the dangers of road accidents. The committee has sent you the statistics which are shown, and they want you to use them to organise a debate/discussion within your institution about the dangers of road accidents involving motor cycles. They have also made other requirements which are listed below.

Recipient

The debate is aimed at young people aged 16–19, especially those who use a cycle or motor cycle to travel to college.

Tasks

(1) Arrange, with others, a survey in the college to identify how the students travel to college.
(2) Arrange, with others, to hold a debate to discuss the issue of road accidents. The motion could be that 'the casuality rates of motor cycle riders is unacceptably high, and motor cycles should be abolished'. Use the statistics which follow, and any other information you can obtain, to justify your case.
(3) Compile a report on the conclusions reached in the debate/discussion. Your report should include a presentation of the details found by the survey carried out in task 1.

Road accidents: casualties*

Great Britain (thousands and rates)

	1961	*1966*	*1971*	*1976*	*1979*	*1980*	*1981*
Road motor vehicles with licences current (thousands)	9966	13286	15478	17832	18624	19210	19309
Index of motor vehicle kilometres[a] (1961 = 100)	100	144	182	208	225	233	227
Casualties from road accidents (thousands)							
Killed	6.9	8.0	7.7	6.6	6.4	6.0	5.8
Seriously injured	84.9	99.8	90.9	79.5	80.5	79.4	78.3
Slightly injured	257.9	284.6	253.5	253.7	247.6	243.3	240.7
Total	349.8	392.5	352.0	339.8	334.5	328.7	324.8
Persons killed or seriously injured by type of road user (thousands)							
Pedestrians							
Under 15	8.3	10.6	11.1	7.9	7.3	6.9	6.5
15–59	7.0	9.3	8.4	7.0	7.8	7.0	7.0
60 and over	7.1	7.9	7.1	5.6	5.6	5.2	4.9
Pedal cyclists							
Under 15	2.9	2.5	2.5	2.1	2.1	2.1	2.1
15 and over	6.9	4.6	3.1	2.8	3.1	3.4	3.4
Casualty rates,[b] by all cyclists		102	122	112	120	110	116
Two-wheeled motor vehicle riders							
Under 17	1.6	2.8	2.4	2.2	1.7	1.8	1.7
17–19	6.2	7.5	4.7	7.9	8.6	9.2	8.9
20 and over	14.6	8.8	6.3	7.8	8.6	9.3	9.2
Casualty rates,[b] all riders	..	304	333	293	274	264	299
Two-wheeled motor vehicle passengers	4.5	3.2	2.1	1.9	2.2	2.3	2.5
Car (including taxi): drivers	10.9	19.5	22.3	19.2	20.0	18.9	19.2
passengers	12.0	20.0	20.3	15.7	15.0	14.3	14.5
Casualty rates,[b] all drivers	..	15	13	9	9	8	9
Other: drivers	3.2	4.7	4.0	2.9	2.7	2.3	2.2
passengers	5.0	5.8	4.2	2.9	2.3	2.1	2.0
All casualties[c]	91.8	107.8	98.6	86.1	86.9	85.4	84.1

[a] Revised series from 1966.
[b] Killed or seriously injured per 100 million kilometres.
[c] Includes type of road user unknown.
Source: Department of Transport
* From *Social Trends, 1983.* (HMSO).

Assignment 9

Television advertising

Post

Assume that you are employed in the sales department of a toy manufacturer.

Organisation

The products of the organisation are distributed throughout the United Kingdom. The company has always distributed most of its products through wholesalers, except two or three selected items aimed at the teenage market, which have been sold through mail order.

Problem

However, in recent months, there has been a sharp decline in the firm's mail order business. The managing director has asked the sales department to investigate the problem, and you have been asked specifically to examine the television advertising and to report any changes.

Recipients

Your report has to be prepared for your immediate supervisor in the sales office.

Tasks

(1) The timing of the advertising is given in the tables which follow. You are required to assess these timings in relation to the charts, and to report on whether you consider them to be appropriate.

(2) Investigate and report on any changes which might have taken place in viewing habits – e.g. home video, breakfast television – which might affect the company's policy on TV advertising.
(3) Design a questionnaire which ascertains the viewing habits of young people aged 16–19.

Advertising on television
Promotion period is October/November/December

	(Times shown using the 24 hour clock)				
Monday to Thursday	16.52	17.36	17.51	18.51	19.22
Friday	18.51	19.21	19.48	20.23	20.57
Saturday	10.26	10.51	11.12	11.43	12.42
Sunday	15.21	16.21	16.59	17.37	18.28

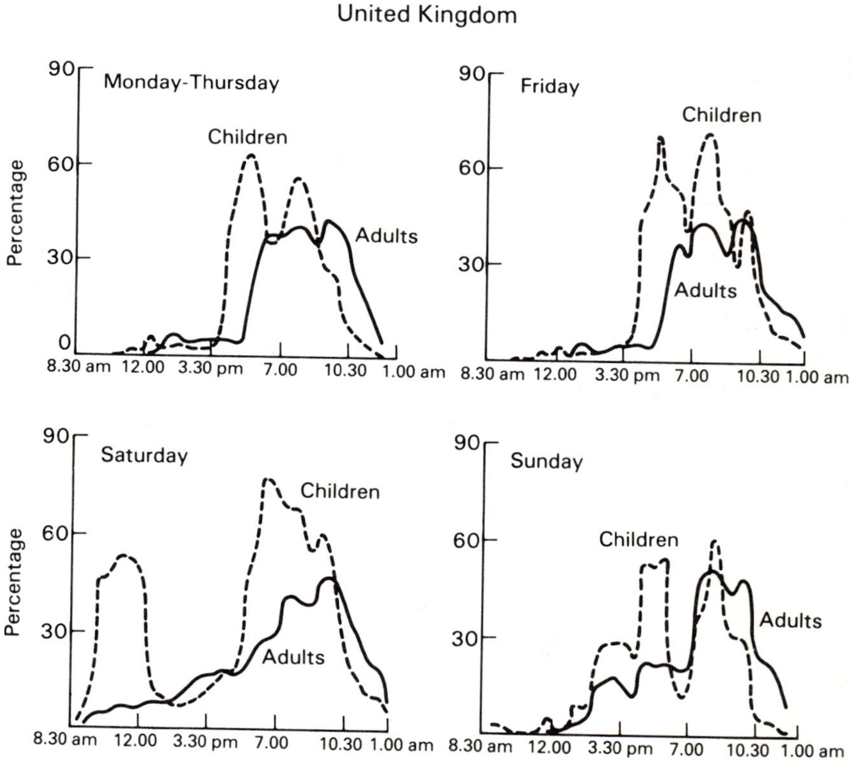

Adults and children watching television: by time of day – weekdays and weekends, February 1981*.

**From Social Trends, 1983 (HMSO)*

Assignment 10

Break-even charts

Post

Assume that you are employed as a junior accountant in the accounting section of a large organisation.

Organisation

The organisation produces a wide range of electrical goods. Each factory within the organisation produces one product.

Problem

The general manager of one of the factories has sent to the accounts office a set of figures which differ from those already acquired. The chief accountant wants a simple method of comparing the two sets of figures; and, to this end, he has asked you to construct two break-even charts which, he feels will immediately illustrate the optimism in the factory manager's figures. Details of his requirements are given below.

Recipients

The chief accountant will use your work in his own report, therefore he would like your contribution to be as concise as possible.

Tasks

Using the information which is given below you are required to:

(1) Complete the table by calculating total costs, average costs, and average revenue.
(2) Construct a chart for each set of data which shows the break-even point for each set.
(3) Use your charts and tables to explain why you think that the factory

manager's figures are too unrealistic. Your explanation should include a definition of the types of cost and a description of the relationship between output and costs and output and price in the long run.

Accounts office figures

Output (units)	*Fixed costs (£)*	*Variable costs (£)*	*Total revenue (£)*
1 000	100 000	500	3 000
10 000	100 000	5 000	30 000
20 000	100 000	10 000	60 000
50 000	100 000	25 000	150 000
100 000	150 000	45 000	250 000
250 000	200 000	150 000	500 000

Complete the following table:

Output	*Total costs*	*Average costs*	*Average revenue*	*Profit/loss*
1 000				
10 000				
20 000				
50 000				
100 000				
250 000				

Factory manager's figures

Output (units)	*Fixed costs (£)*	*Variable costs (£)*	*Total revenue (£)*
1 000	100 000	500	3 000
10 000	100 000	5 000	30 000
20 000	100 000	10 000	60 000
50 000	100 000	25 000	150 000
100 000	100 000	50 000	300 000
250 000	100 000	125 000	750 000

Complete the following table:

Output	*Total costs*	*Average costs*	*Average revenue*	*Profit/loss*
1 000				
10 000				
20 000				
50 000				
100 000				
250 000				

Assignment 11

Health care

Post

Assume that you are an administrator in a hospital.

Organisation

The hospital is part of the National Health Service; and the employees are very conscious of the needs of the patients and the limitation of resources.

Problem

A letter, published in the local press, is highly critical of the services of the hospital, and included in the criticism is a suggestion that individual patients should pay their own hospital fees. You have been asked to draft a reply to the letter.

Recipients

Your immediate supervisor will revise and edit your work, but the main substance of your draft will be published in the local newspaper.

Tasks

(1) Using the table below calculate the average cost for both males and females; and compare the average cost with the cost for each age group.
(2) Using your results from Task 1 describe the variation in the health needs within the population, and explain why such a variation exists.
(3) Briefly comment on how a NHS hospital is funded, and contrast such funding with the suggestion that each individual should pay for their own health care.

National Health Service
Annual cost per person by age and by sex

(£ per person)

Age	*Males*	*Females*
Under 1	311	254
1–4	117	103
5–15	73	66
16–24	75	74
25–44	82	86
45–64	127	121
65–74	268	244
75+	507	623

Source: Central Statistical Office.
Notes: The figures exclude maternity, administration, and capital costs.

Population distribution of the region

(thousands)

Age	*Males*	*Females*
Under 1	4	4
1–4	18	17
5–15	45	43
16–24	41	40
25–44	67	66
45–64	64	69
65–74	20	27
75+	8	17

Source: Central Statistical Office.

Assignment 12

Visit to London

Post

Assume that you are the secretary of a college political studies society.

Organisation

The society arranges lectures and visits on political subjects. It is a thriving group and has 20 to 25 active members.

Problem

The society is short of funds, and it appears that many members cannot afford the cost of the society's annual visit to the Houses of Parliament. You, as secretary, have been asked to find out the cost and the time of various modes of travel.

Recipients

Your report has to be prepared for the next meeting of the society.

Tasks

(1) Obtain the information to complete the table given to show the time taken by each mode, and the total and individual cost of each mode.
(2) Construct a bar chart which shows both the mean average cost per mile and the total time for each mode.
(3) Draw up a timetable which allows a six-hour visit to London. The six hours is made up of meal 1.5 hrs, Parliament 2.5 hrs, and free time 2 hrs.

Visit to Houses of Parliament

Starting point is the college.

Copy and complete the following table. Show the cheapest quotations in all cases.

Mode of travel	*Journey time*	*Total cost* (£)	*Individual cost* (£)		
			15	*20*	*25*
Coach 15 seater 20 seater 25 seater					
Rail Party rate 15 20 25 Cheap day Ordinary					
Minibus hire 15 Cost per day Mileage charge Parking charge Totals					
Minibus hire 20 Cost per day Mileage charge Parking charge Totals					
Minibus hire 25 Cost per day Mileage charge Parking charge Totals					

Individual cost column should show the cost for each individual for party sizes of 15, 20 or 25. The price of the coach, the rail fare and the cost of the minibus could vary according to the size required. These variations should be shown in the table.

Assignment 13

Consumers' expenditure

Post

Assume that you are employed as a clerical officer in the local authority.

Organisation

The local authority has instituted a research and development unit. The aim of the unit is to assess local and national economic and social trends, and to advise elected officials on such trends. You are a new recruit to the unit.

Problem

The supervisor of the unit has found that there is no centralised collection of local statistics. He has decided that the unit should analyse the government's published statistics and collate those which refer specifically to the local region. You have been given the tasks of collating and analysing data on consumers' expenditure.

Recipient

Your work has to be submitted directly to your supervisor.

Tasks

(1) Examine the table below and, by research, obtain more up to date statistics on consumers' expenditure.
(2) Using 1976 as a base calculate an index of each heading – food, drink and tobacco, housing and fuel, durables and vehicles, other, total – for: (i) your region, (ii) your country and (iii) the United Kingdom; and construct a table which enables comparisons to be made.
(3) Obtain information on regional unemployment since 1976, and construct a chart which compares the trends in unemployment with trends in consumers' expenditure.

Consumers' expenditure*

((£) million)

	Total	*Food drink and tobacco*	*Housing and fuel*	*Durables and vehicles*	*Other*
1976					
United Kingdom	74 952	22 672	14 111	12 801	25 368
North	3 849	1 303	653	660	1 233
Yorkshire and Humberside	6 116	1 957	1 055	1 055	2 049
East Midlands	4 763	1 510	896	863	1 494
East Anglia	2 297	657	452	429	759
South East	25 838	6 982	5 292	4 281	9 283
South West	5 579	1 599	1 132	1 084	1 764
West Midlands	6 528	2 082	1 224	1 162	2 060
North West	8 224	2 641	1 544	1 309	2 730
England	63 194	18 731	12 248	10 843	21 372
Wales	3 452	1 141	552	615	1 144
Scotland	6 525	2 231	1 032	1 028	2 234
Northern Ireland	1 781	569	279	315	618
1977					
United Kingdom	86 001	26 102	16 543	14 406	28 950
North	4 360	1 510	760	707	1 392
Yorkshire and Humberside	7 048	2 306	1 207	1 174	2 361
East Midlands	5 327	1 720	1 048	943	1 616
East Anglia	2 685	783	560	500	842
South East	29 632	7 975	6 150	4 868	10 639
South West	6 338	1 863	1 308	1 168	1 999
West Midlands	7 631	2 419	1 478	1 328	2 406
North West	9 396	3 029	1 797	1 480	3 090
England	72 417	21 596	14 308	12 168	24 345
Wales	3 982	1 281	679	715	1 307
Scotland	7 529	2 575	1 189	1 178	2 587
Northern Ireland	2 073	650	367	345	711
1978					
United Kingdom	98 947	29 066	18 729	17 241	33 911
North	5 039	1 667	884	862	1 626
Yorkshire and Humberside	8 003	2 610	1 358	1 329	2 706
East Midlands	6 194	1 926	1 178	1 153	1 937
East Anglia	3 170	902	652	600	1 016
South East	33 905	8 843	6 868	5 870	12 324
South West	7 124	2 054	1 460	1 274	2 336
West Midlands	9 011	2 752	1 753	1 646	2 860
North West	10 904	3 321	2 058	1 867	3 658
England	83 350	24 075	16 211	14 601	28 463
Wales	4 566	1 429	787	832	1 518
Scotland	8 645	2 858	1 321	1 429	3 037
Northern Ireland	2 386	704	410	379	893
1979					
United Kingdom	116 717	33 260	22 003	21 224	40 230
North	6 035	1 931	1 075	1 065	1 964
Yorkshire and Humberside	9 311	2 950	1 597	1 554	3 210
East Midlands	7 457	2 199	1 331	1 496	2 431
East Anglia	3 773	1 050	758	726	1 239
South East	39 831	10 122	8 025	7 262	14 422
South West	8 331	2 327	1 728	1 554	2 722
West Midlands	10 648	3 125	2 099	2 045	3 379
North West	13 039	3 856	2 459	2 325	4 399
England	98 425	27 560	19 072	18 027	33 766
Wales	5 384	1 675	920	1 013	1 776
Scotland	10 056	3 201	1 514	1 728	3 613
Northern Ireland	2 852	824	497	456	1 075

Source: Central Statistical Office. * Table from *Social Trends*, 1983 (HMSO).

Assignment 14

Accounting information and the microcomputer

Post

Assume that you are an applicant for a post as clerical assistant/ accountant.

Organisation

The organisation is a small but successful business, Hire-It, which sells and hires out tools and DIY equipment. The business is owned by one person who has always relied on professional accountants to keep the accounting records. The owner now feels confident enough to employ someone within the organisation who could act as accountant and general office manager. The proprietor is also considering the purchase of a microcomputer which will be used to keep accounting and stock records.

Problem

You have applied for the job, and the proprietor has presented you with details of some typical trading transactions. Using this information you are asked to complete the series of tasks which are given below.

Recipient

Your assignment will, of course, be examined by the proprietor of the business; but the results will also be shown to the professional accountant.

Tasks

Using the information below you are required to:

(1) Write a concise report which describes the impact of technological change on accounting functions; and give examples of how a microcomputer could be used in this type of organisation.
(2) Examine the information below and list the files which would have to be created if the data is to be processed electronically. Show the interrelationship between the files.
(3) Compile a list of commercial software which might be appropriate for this type of business; and review the advantages and disadvantages of purchasing 'ready made' programs.

The following is a list of typical trading transactions of Hire-It.

Day	*Transaction*	*Amount* (£)
1	Capital paid in and lodged in bank	4 000
1	Purchased tools by cheque	814
2	Purchased goods from James on credit	600
3	Purchased goods from Rust on credit	260
4	Paid rent by cheque	122
5	Cash sales	97
5	Hired goods – cash received	150
6	Sold goods to Smart on credit	160
6	Paid part-time wages in cash	46
8	Paid James by cheque (– 5% discount)	570
9	Sold goods to Wood on credit	364
9	Hired goods to Gold on credit	300
10	Paid Rust by cheque	260
11	Paid petty expenses in cash	20
12	Hired goods – cash received	315
12	Cash sales	212
13	Paid part-time wages in cash	46
15	Cash purchases	128
15	Sold goods to Wate on credit	143
16	Paid carriage on purchases	15
17	Purchased from Wild goods on credit	106
17	Received cash from Smart (– 5% discount)	152
18	Paid insurance for next half-year	163
19	Hired goods – cash received	364
19	Cash sales	261
20	Paid part-time wages in cash	46
22	Paid petty expenses in cash	23
23	Purchased goods for cash	186
23	Wate returned goods value	78
24	Sold goods to Smart on credit	468
24	Sold goods to Wate on credit	239
25	Paid electricity bill by cheque – the bill was for the previous quarter	107
26	Hired goods – cash received	294
26	Cash sales	224
27	Paid part-time wages in cash	46
29	Paid cash into bank	1 100

Assignment 15

The flow of financial information

Post

Assume that you are employed in the accounting section of a well established private company.

Organisation

The company owns a chain of seaside hotels. Although over the years some standard elements have been introduced into the accounting system, each hotel has been run as an autonomous unit; and the company's management consider that many of the existing accounting procedures are out of date.

Problem

The company wants to introduce a comprehensive information processing system which is based on a commercial software package designed for a small business computer. Each hotel will remain independent but will have to use the new standard system of information processing. A meeting of the hotel managers has been arranged to discuss the issue, and you have been asked to start the discussion by giving an oral presentation along the lines outlined below.

Recipients

There will be about 20 to 25 people attending the meeting. However, prior to the meeting the director responsible for accounting in the company has asked you to discuss your presentation with him. He wishes to see the notes and the flow-chart you have prepared for the oral presentation.

Tasks

(1) Outline the main business activities which you consider are common to all of the hotels.
(2) Describe, briefly, the influence of technological change upon the type and methods of collection of financial information in the hotel industry. Your description should include an outline of the organisation's structure and its internal communication system.
(3) Using the table below as a framework add examples of accounting functions in an hotel to each stage of the flow of information. Then construct a flowchart which illustrates the way in which accounting functions are linked to the company's activities.

The flow of financial information

Stages in the flow of information	*Examples of types of activity*	*Examples of accounting procedures*
Collecting information		
Recording	Bookings by	
	Post	
	Telephone	
	Desk	
	Purchases	
	Other costs/expenses	
Operating with information		
Sorting	Room allocation	
Collating	Client's bill	
Checking	Bar records	
Storing	Restaurant stock	
Application of information		
Feedback	Performance measurement	
Presentation	Pricing structure	
Interpretation	Profitability assessment	
Development	Planning	

The table is a framework which gives some examples of the types of business operations which occur in hotels, and it shows the stage at which these operations occur in the flow of information. You are required to make the table as comprehensive as possible by adding further examples of business activities and by giving examples of accounting procedures which relate to them. For instance 'performance measurement' can be undertaken by financial ratios which in turn are linked to the final accounts. Having expanded the table you are then required to construct a flowchart which shows the inter-relationship of the various activities and the accounting functions.

Assignment 16

Cash flow

Post

Assume that you are the treasurer of a students' union.

Organisation

The Students' Union is a thriving organisation which runs sporting and social functions. It derives its income from a variety of sources such as subscriptions, dances and a snack bar.

Problem

The students responsible for the running of the snack bar manage their own finances and they want to purchase a new microwave oven which will cost £1 550. The union executive feel that there is inefficiency in the financial management of the snack bar; and they have decided that the purchase of new equipment must come from any surpluses derived from the snack bar operation. You have been asked to analyse the finances of the snack bar and to prepare a cash flow statement to see whether it is feasible to purchase the microwave oven.

Recipients

Your report has to be prepared for the next meeting of the students' union executive. The executive is made up of representatives from the whole student body.

Tasks

(1) You are required to use the information in the table to prepare a cash flow statement for each month of the next financial year.
(2) Compile a report which illustrates how savings might be made.

Your report should draw attention to those costs which are fixed and those which might be controlled.
(3) Explain, in your report, the importance of the accurate control of information.

The Students' Union. Estimates of monthly cash position for the next financial period
(based on the records of the previous financial year)

Receipts	*Food sales (£)*	*Drink sales (£)*	*Juke box gaming m/c (£)*
January	260	115	32
February	321	189	56
March	298	176	40
April	272	188	49
May	290	201	33
June	132	156	21
July	23	51	10
August	5	12	2
September	204	189	41
October	391	244	63
November	365	216	56
December	242	178	32

Expenditure	*Purchases food (£)*	*Purchases drink (£)*	*Labour cost (£)*	*Overheads (£)*
January	150	100	80	40
February	145	96	80	40
March	136	102	80	40
April	169	91	80	40
May	150	100	80	40
June	198	123	80	40
July	100	83	80	40
August	142	96	80	40
September	169	122	80	40
October	125	87	80	40
November	146	102	80	40
December	168	75	80	40

Notes:
1. The purchases listed above refer to orders placed, the actual bills are paid two months later.
2. You have discovered that there is no system of stock control or systematic re-ordering scheme. Consequently stocks were often running out, and some items were overstocked.
3. The wages are paid to a part-time bar attendant, and are paid in cash every week.
4. All of the receipts are cash receipts.
5. The cash/bank balance at the beginning of the period was £518.

The students' union executive will decide whether it is feasible to purchase the microwave oven on the basis of your report. Your report, therefore, should include a recommendation which can be justified.

Assignment 17

Comparison of performance

Post

Assume that you are employed as a clerical assistant in the office of a garage.

Organisation

The garage is used to service and repair motor vehicles as well as selling petrol and motor car products. The business is owned by one man, and in recent years it has been very successful.

Problem

During the past three weeks the office manager has been ill, and you have had to undertake his duties as well as your own. The owner of the garage is preoccupied with the purchase of another business, and he has asked you to examine the following balance sheets from two businesses which he is interested in. The details of his requirements are outlined below.

Recipient

The owner has never formally studied accountancy, and he is looking to you for guidance on interpreting the accounting information.

Tasks

Using the accounting information below you are required to:

(1) Calculate appropriate financial ratios, and briefly explain their significance.

(2) Explain the concepts implicit in the measurement of profit and the valuation of assets.
(3) Briefly report on your assessment of the two businesses, and list the additional information you would need to make a more accurate assessment.

Balance sheet A
Balance sheet of —— as at 31 December 19xx

	(£)	(£)
Fixed assets		
Premises at cost		15 000
Plant and machinery at cost	51 300	
less depreciation	25 200	26 100
Motor vehicle at cost	7 500	
less depreciation	3 600	3 900
Long-term capital		45 000
Current assets		
Stock in trade	69 300	
Trade debtors	48 150	
Bank balance	1 500	
	118 950	
deduct *Current liabilities*		
Trade creditors	78 450	
Working capital	40 500	
deduct Reserve	3 000	37 500
Net worth of the company		£82 500
Financed by:		
45000 ordinary shares @ £1 each		45 000
Profit and loss account		19 500
General reserve		6 000
Loan		12 000
		£82 500

Details from the profit and loss account:

(1) Annual sales/revenue for the period £355 500
(2) Gross profit £ 61 500
(3) Net profit before taxation £ 9 000

Balance sheet B
Balance sheet of —— as at 31 December 19xx

	(£)	(£)
Fixed assets		
Premises at cost		25 000
Plant and machinery at cost	42 300	
less depreciation	10 575	31 725
Motor vehicle at cost	6 500	
less depreciation	4 875	1 625
Long-term capital		58 350
Current assets		
Stock in trade	46 800	
Trade debtors	92 450	
Bank balance	800	
	140 050	
deduct *Current liabilities*		
Trade creditors	82 360	
Working capital	57 690	
deduct Reserve	5 000	52 690
Net worth of the company		£111 040
Financed by:		
70 000 ordinary shares £1 each		70 000
Profit and loss account		17 000
General reserve		4 500
Loan		19 540
		£111 040

Details from the profit and loss account:

(1) Annual sales/revenue for the period	£298 000
(2) Gross profit	£ 57 300
(3) Net profit before taxation	£ 12 000

Assignment 18

The sports and social club

Post

Assume that you are a member of a sports social club, and that you have just been elected treasurer.

Organisation

The club is very active. In addition to sporting fixtures, the club committee runs a very successful bar, and organises dances and other social events. It employs a full-time manager to run the bar, as well as several part-time people.

Problem

There are rumours that the bar manager is misappropriating the club's funds. As part of the process of investigation you have been asked to undertake the tasks listed below.

Recipients

You are to report to the club committee at an emergency meeting.

Tasks

(1) From the list of balances you are required to prepare a profit and loss account for the previous six months trading and a balance sheet as at that date.
(2) You are required to comment on the trading position, and to give reasons for your conclusions. Prepare a list of any additional information which would help you to assess the position.

(3) You must be prepared to explain how the valuation of stocks at the year end can affect profitability; and to make suggestions of how the levels of existing stock should be checked and controlled.

From the following list of balances you are required to prepare a profit and loss account and a balance sheet for the six-month period 1 April to 30 September.

The sports and social club

	(£)
Cash	240
Debtors (club members)	126
Creditors	1 340
Motor vehicle	1 600
Purchases	25 420
Purchases returns	172
Wages and salaries	5 300
Stock 1 April	5 400
Bank interest and charges	105
General expenses	2 630
Bar sales	32 490
Food sales	2 630
Income from events	1 400
Income from subscriptions	7 540
Income from machines	1 610
Bad debts	340
Rent, rates and insurance	1 900
Discounts received	450
Motor vehicle expenses	320
Fruit machines rental	500
Bank overdraft	1 200

You are given the following additional information:

(1) The stock at the end of the period was valued at £3 250. This figure is an estimate based on a quick survey.
(2) Rent, rates and insurance and the rental on the fruit machines are payments which have been made for the 12-month period beginning 1 April.
(3) Members' subscriptions are paid annually on 1 January; it would appear that £30 is still outstanding.
(4) £25 should be provided for estimated bank interest and charges for the quarter 1 July–30 September.
(5) Wages which have accrued amount to £23.
(6) The net profit for the 12 months ending 31 March was £5 390.

Assignment 19

Seaside restaurant

Post

Assume that a friend has inherited a seaside restaurant; and he, knowing of your knowledge of accounts, has invited you to help him manage the business.

Organisation

The restaurant has been operating successfully for several years, but during recent months the aunt has been ill and its trading position has declined.

Problem

Your friend is aware that the restaurant has been neglected; and he wants you to examine the books, and to comment on the state of the business.

Recipient

The recipient of your report will be your friend who owns the business. He has a weak knowledge of accounts.

Tasks

(1) From the trial balance prepare a trading, profit and loss account for the year ended 31 December 19xx and a balance sheet as at that date.
(2) Comment on the trading position of the business.
(3) Comment specifically on the expenditure on wages, staff meals, and telephones; and indicate how these costs might be controlled.

From the following trial balance you are required to prepare a profit and loss account and a balance sheet for the year ended 31 December 19xx.

Seaside restaurant

	(£)	(£)
Capital		40 000
Electricity	2 100	
Rent and rates	1 950	
Stock at 1 January	520	
Discounts received		150
Sundry receipts		75
China and cutlery	1 200	
Purchases	19 430	
Purchases returns		120
Premises (freehold)	28 000	
Stationery	710	
Furniture	2 630	
Cash in hand	40	
Creditors		1 310
Wages and salaries	12 600	
Staff meals	1 500	
Postage	90	
Telephone	560	
Drawings	2 200	
Sales		44 345
Kitchen equipment	5 000	
Cash at bank	6 060	
Professional charges	640	
Miscellaneous expenses	770	
	£86 000	£86 000

Notes:

1. The stock at 31 December was valued at £202.
2. The net profit to sales ratio in the previous trading year was 10.5%.
3. The following are items taken from the trial balance of the previous trading year:

Sales	£49 640
Staff meals	£ 975
Telephone	£ 320
Wages	£ 9 300

Assignment 20

Ratio analysis

Post

Assume that you are employed as a trainee accountant in a firm of professional accountants.

Organisation

The partners in the firm where you work encourage their professional employees to take an active part in the local Junior Chamber of Commerce.

Problem

There are many new members in the Junior Chamber of Commerce who know very little about accountancy; and, as part of an educational programme which is designed for the exchange of knowledge and ideas between the members, you have been invited to present a talk entitled 'A layman's guide to interpreting accounting information'.

Recipients

Many of the members are, like you, just starting a career in business and commerce; and they represent a wide cross-section of local business and public service. Consequently your talk should be kept simple yet be as comprehensive as possible.

Tasks

One of the senior partners in your firm has advised you to concentrate on ratio analysis and to prepare your contribution along the following lines.

(1) Distinguish between different types of organisation, and at the same time outline the main characteristics which are common to all organisations. This is to show that there is common ground between the members.

(2) Using the fictitious final accounts below explain the significance and limitations of ratio analysis.
(3) The fictitious example is of a manufacturing organisation. Be prepared to give illustrations of how ratio analysis could be applied to other types of business activity.

Trading, profit and loss account for XYZ plc for the year ending 31 December 19xx

	(£)	(£)
Income from sales		232 000
Costs		
Raw materials	122 000	
Wages (direct)	68 000	
Fuel and power	6 000	196 000
Gross profit on trading		36 000
Gross profit (b/d)	36 000	
Income from other sources	5 000	41 000
Expenses not incurred in manufacturing		
Debenture interest	800	
Directors' fees	8 000	
Depreciation		
Plant and machinery	5 600	
Motor vehicle	600	
Wages and salaries	12 000	
Rent and rates	1 500	
Hire of equipment	1 500	
Light and heat	1 000	
Advertising	1 200	
Post and telephone	750	
Other expenses	2 050	35 000
Net profit before taxation		6 000

Appropriation account

		(£)
Net profit (b/d)		6 000
Taxation (40%)		2 400
Net profit after tax		3 600
Net profit after tax	3 600	
Balance from previous year	13 500	17 100
Deduct appropriations		
Dividends proposed	3 000	
Transfers to reserve	1 100	4 100
Balance on the profit and loss account		13 000

Balance sheet of XYZ plc as at 31 December 19xx

	(£)	(£)
Fixed assets		
Premises at cost		10 000
Plant/machinery at cost	34 200	
less depreciation	16 800	17 400
Motor vehicle at cost	5 000	
less depreciation	2 400	2 600
Long-term capital		30 000
Current assets		
Stock in trade	46 200	
Trade debtors	32 100	
Balance at bank	1 000	
	79 300	
deduct Current liabilities		
Trade creditors	52 300	
Working capital	27 000	
deduct reserve for taxation	2 000	25 000
Net worth of the Company		55 000
Financed by		
Issued share capital:		
Ordinary shares (20 000 @ £1 each)		20 000
Preference shares 5% (10 000 @ £1 each)		10 000
Profit and loss account		13 000
General reserve		4 000
Loan		
10% Debentures		8 000
		55 000

Note: You will probably find it useful to compile a fictitious set of final accounts for XYZ plc for the period following this set, so that the value of ratios in making intra-firm comparisons can be illustrated in your talk.

Answers to diagnostic test (Exercise 1.1)

(*a*) 184	(*b*) 22	(*c*) 49
(*d*) 406	(*e*) 17	(*f*) 329
(*g*) 3819	(*h*) 89	(*i*) 140
(*j*) 24	(*k*) −20	(*l*) −18
(*m*) 45	(*n*) 54	(*o*) 99
(*p*) 30	(*q*) 40	(*r*) 30
(*s*) −12	(*t*) 30	(*u*) −14
(*v*) −600	(*w*) 1911	(*x*) −1716